# The Witches' Almanac

Spring 2013 — Spring 2014

CONTAINING pictorial and explicit delineations of the
magical phases of the Moon together with information about astrological
portents of the year to come and various aspects of occult knowledge
enabling all who read to improve their lives in the old manner.

The Witches' Almanac, Ltd.

Publishers    Providence, Rhode Island
*www.TheWitchesAlmanac.com*

Address all inquiries and information to
THE WITCHES' ALMANAC, LTD.
P.O. Box 1292
Newport, RI   02840-9998

10-ISBN: 0-9824323-7-2
13-ISBN: 978-0-9824323-7-2

ISSN: 1522-3183

First Printing June 2012

Printed in the United States of America

Printed on recycled paper

Established 1971 by Elizabeth Pepper

# Preface

WITCHES SEE THINGS DIFFERENTLY. When we think of friends, we ordinarily think of those people in our lives whom we can lean on, as well as those who can rely on us, in times of personal need. Support is common between friends – advice and a good ear are among the traits that true friends share.

As a witch, we are not so limited to our realm of friends. A witch's friends are deemed from the relationships we have nurtured with the Mighty Dead, our animal familiars, land spirits, nature spirits, and even cosmic intelligences. But it is a rare time, when we are blessed with a mutual understanding of what friendship means between two creatures of nature. Some of us have been lucky enough to recognize a friend or familiar from a past life, fortunate enough to rekindle that relationship and develop the bond to a greater depth because of this understanding.

As a practitioner of the delicate arts, we also need to know that assistance offered or given to a friend means support on all planes of existence. Being magic-workers, we are aware of these subtle differences between the physical and ethereal planes, as well as the other realms, and as such, we need to be prepared to flaw-lessly bridge them when a friend is in need.

We are gifted with knowledge that others do not have, but with this insight comes a responsibility to our friends and to the world around us.

# ～∞ HOLIDAYS ∞～

## Spring 2013 to Spring 2014

March 20 . . . . . . . . . . . . . . . . . . . . . . . . . . . . . . . . . . . Vernal Equinox
April 1 . . . . . . . . . . . . . . . . . . . . . . . . . . . . . . . . . . . All Fools' Day
April 30 . . . . . . . . . . . . . . . . . . . . . . . . . . . . . . . . Walpurgis Night
May 1 . . . . . . . . . . . . . . . . . . . . . . . . . . . . . . . . . . . . . . . Beltane
May 8 . . . . . . . . . . . . . . . . . . . . . . . . . . . . . . . White Lotus Day
May 9, 11, 13 . . . . . . . . . . . . . . . . . . . . . . . . . . . . . Lemuria
May 25 . . . . . . . . . . . . . . . . . . . . . . . . . . . . . . . . . . Vesak Day
May 29 . . . . . . . . . . . . . . . . . . . . . . . . . . . . . . Oak Apple Day
June 5 . . . . . . . . . . . . . . . . . . . . . . . . . . . Night of the Watchers
June 21 . . . . . . . . . . . . . . . . . . . . . . . . . . . . . Summer Solstice
June 24 . . . . . . . . . . . . . . . . . . . . . . . . . . . . . . Midsummer
July 23 . . . . . . . . . . . . . . . . . . . . . . Ancient Egyptian New Year
July 31 . . . . . . . . . . . . . . . . . . . . . . . . . . . Lughnassad Eve
August 1 . . . . . . . . . . . . . . . . . . . . . . . . . . . . . . . . . Lammas
August 13 . . . . . . . . . . . . . . . . . . . . . . . . . . . . Diana's Day
September 9 . . . . . . . . . . . . . . . . . . . . . . . . . Ganesh Festival
September 22 . . . . . . . . . . . . . . . . . . . . . . . . Autumnal Equinox
October 31 . . . . . . . . . . . . . . . . . . . . . . . . . . . . . . . Samhain Eve
November 1 . . . . . . . . . . . . . . . . . . . . . . . . . . . . . . . Hallowmas
November 16 . . . . . . . . . . . . . . . . . . . . . . . . . . . . . Hecate Night
December 17 . . . . . . . . . . . . . . . . . . . . . . . . . . . . . . . Saturnalia
December 21 . . . . . . . . . . . . . . . . . . . . . . . . . . . Winter Solstice
January 9 . . . . . . . . . . . . . . . . . . . . . . . . . . . . . . Feast of Janus
February 1 . . . . . . . . . . . . . . . . . . . . . . . . . . . . . . . Oimelc Eve
February 2 . . . . . . . . . . . . . . . . . . . . . . . . . . . . . Candlemas
February 15 . . . . . . . . . . . . . . . . . . . . . . . . . . . . . . . Lupercalia
March 1 . . . . . . . . . . . . . . . . . . . . . . . . . . . . . . . . . Matronalia
March 19 . . . . . . . . . . . . . . . . . . . . . . . . . . . . . . Minerva's Day

Art Director . . . . . . . . . . . . . . . Karen Marks

Astrologer . . . . . . . . . . . . Dikki-Jo Mullen

Climatologist . . . . . . . . . . . . . . Tom C. Lang

Cover Art and Design. . . Ogmios MacMerlin

Production Consultant . . . . . . . Robin Antoni

Sales . . . . . . . . . . . . . . . . . . . . Ellen Lynch

Shipping, Bookkeeping . . . . . D. Lamoureux

ANDREW THEITIC
Executive Editor

JEAN MARIE WALSH
Associate Editor

JUDIKA ILLES
Copy Editor

# CONTENTS

# The White Witch

"O What have you seen, my son,
  my son,
That your eyes are so wild and bright?
Or what have you heard in the
  eerie woods,
'Twixt the gloaming and the night?"

"I have met a witch, a white white witch,
My mother, mother dear;
The glamour of earth is on my eyes,
And its music in my ear.

"For we are deafen'd by angry words,
Are blinded by tears of woe,
But she has garner'd the secret joys
That only the genii know;—

"Has learn'd from the voice of the
  fern-hid stream
Where all sweet thoughts abide,
And the violets have told her how
  they dream
In the quiet eventide;

"And they fancy, mother, the
world above
Where the baby cloudlets play
Yearns down to the earth in mystic love
That shall never pass away.

"The greenwood knows it; of this
  sweet thought

Its murmuring tunes are made,
And the strange wild tale that is
  ever wrought
Through its sunshine and its shade.

"And the holy moon,
  as she moves along
From star to star on high,
Pours forth her light as a bridal song
And a tender lullaby.

"O mother, my mother, mother dear,
Who may the white witch be!
She has heard the things we
  cannot hear,
She has seen what we cannot see;

"The beauty that comes in
  fitful gleams,
That comes, but will not stay,
The music that steals across
  our dreams
From a region far away;

"What vainly I sought in pain
  and doubt,
The light, the form, the tone,
At a single glance she has found
  them out,
And made them all her own.

"And with all the music we
  cannot hear,
The beauty we cannot see,
O mother, mother, my mother dear,
She has wrought a charm on me."

*– from* Studies in Verse,
*by Charles Grant, 1875*

# Yesterday, Today and Tomorrow

by Timi Chasen

HOPPING IN CIRCLES. An interesting new theory on crop circle formation has recently emerged. It seems wallabies are rather fond of the poppy plants grown in Australia for the international pharmaceutical market. The wallabies sneak in at night, consume the poppies, and proceed to hop around in circles until they become exhausted and collapse. They wander off in the morning, leaving the poppy farmers to scratch their heads. How wallabies may have learned fractal patterns has yet to be explained.

 MUDDLED MOOSE & LOADED LEMURS. Wallabies aren't the only wild animals caught altering their states. Moose in Sweden are known to scavenge for fermented apples. Sometimes they have one too many and stumble into populated areas – one recently became stuck in a tree and required the intervention of local law enforcement. Meanwhile, ringtailed lemurs are exploiting a toxin produced by millipedes. They bite the bugs to induce a defense response, then rub the secretions on their fur. The secretions are an effective bug repellent, but an even more effective hallucinogen. Who knows what other substances these wild animals are using while we're not watching?

WELCOME HOME. In 1990, Congress passed the Native American Graves Protection and Repatriation Act, designed to return culturally significant artifacts and human remains to the tribes from which they originated. Because the original law, which sought to reconcile the rights of Native people with potential scientific significance, required proof of a direct tribal link, remains and artifacts often lay unclaimed in museums for decades. Two years ago, this law was modified to make it easier for tribes to claim the remains of their ancestors and repatriate important cultural items.

Now, instead of being required to prove a direct link, Native peoples have claim over any ancient remains found near known tribal sites. Museums are kicking into high gear to comply with the new rules, reaching out to tribes and conducting genetic testing on remains to determine origin and make the process of repatriation that much easier. While some worry the new looser rules will compromise scientific inquiry or may result in remains being returned to the wrong groups, others hail it as a boon to Native rights. Many times (but by no means in all cases) the remains have spent years in museum basements, never being examined or investigated. Now they will be coming home to rest. Native American leaders have promised to treat all returned remains – even those of unknown provenance – with the same respect afforded their most revered ancestors.

## REVELATION AT ROCCAPELAGO.

An amazing find has been unearthed in the Italian mountain town of Roccapelago. There, in the crypt of the Church of the Conversion of St. Paul, a veritable mountain of human remains – many of them naturally mummified –

has been discovered. Also found among the remains were scattered jewelry, religious medallions, and, perhaps most exciting, a rare "lettera componenda". This artifact is a letter written by a church official which promises the bearer spiritual perks in exchange for prayer. The letter reads, in part:

*"and he who carries it on him will be free from the Devil and will not die bad death. Carried it on her the pregnant woman will give birth without danger. In the house where this Revelation lives there will be no illusion of bad things before her death will see the Glorious Virgin Mary Amen"*

KARATS ON CARROTS. A woman in Sweden had given up hope of ever finding her diamond ring, misplaced while baking Christmas cookies with her family. Sixteen years later, however, she found it, wrapped snug around a carrot she pulled from her garden. The family surmises the ring became mixed in with vegetable scraps, which were then composted and spread on the garden. Money may not grow on trees, but sometimes diamonds grow on carrots.

**LOCATION, LOCATION, LOCATION.** The Roman Temple of Mithras, excavated in London in 1952, will be removed from its current location at Walbrook Square and returned to its original location. The Temple's current location was purchased for development by Bloomburg LP, precipitating the deconstruction of the temple. The temple will be restored faithfully sometime next year.

**MYSTERY AT STONEHENGE.**
Thanks to modern scientific techniques and the perseverance of curious minds, the bluestones of Stonehenge have been definitively sourced. The bluestones were examined microscopically and crosschecked against a database of samples from across the country in order to establish their origin. The stones were quarried in south Wales at an outcrop known as Craig Rhos-y-Felin. The bluestones were then transported roughly 200 miles to their current location, either by human transport or glacial forces – exactly how is one of the many mysteries which remain unanswered about the famous monument.

**COME OUT, COME OUT, WHEREVER YOU ARE.** It's been a tough year for cryptozoologists. First, the Pangboche hand, supposedly that of a yeti, was shown conclusively through DNA testing to be nothing more than an oversized human hand. Next, footage of a sea monster off the coast of Alaska was widely panned as hardly convincing. Finally, the body of a "chupacabra" found on a Texas golf course turned out to be an anomalous hairless raccoon instead. Will all this negative feedback

stop these intrepid explorers into the world of unknown fauna? Probably not. A good cryptozoologist knows that the absence of evidence is not evidence of absence.

A VIEW OF THE MOON. In October of 2010, the China National Space Administration launched Chang'e 2, an unmanned lunar probe named for the fabled Lady of the Moon. The probe is expected to remain in lunar orbit studying the lunar surface through the end of 2012 to prepare the way for Chang'e 3, which should land on the moon sometime in 2013.

TWO ANCIENT BABYLONIANS WALK INTO A BAR... In 1976, archeologists working in Iraq uncovered a badly damaged tablet in cuneiform script dating from around thirty-five thousand years ago. Curious minds have since translated what remains of the tablet. Their results, published in the scholarly journal *Iraq*, seem to reveal the world's oldest collection of jokes. Decidedly bawdy in nature, the jokes or riddles address such subjects as sex and beer. One of the incomplete

jokes has garnered quite a bit of attention in the popular press:

*...of your mother is by the one who has intercourse with her. What/who is it?* [No answer]

Could this be, as some have suggested, the world's oldest "Yo Mama" joke? It certainly qualifies as a crass joke at the expense of a matronly figure, but many questions remain to be answered in regards to the tablet. Perhaps these are not even jokes after all, but short moral tales designed to improve civil behavior. Whether intended as jokes or not, we are certainly getting a kick out of them now!

# Drawing Down the Moon

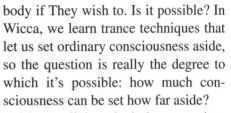

IN WICCA, "Drawing Down the Moon" (commonly abbreviated as DDM) refers to the ritual of bringing the Goddess into the body of the High Priestess, so that She may speak to the assembled Witches using the High Priestess's voice. Although the moon is specified, the ritual may be used to summon any Goddess, not just a lunar Goddess. Similarly, Drawing Down the Sun (DDS) may be used to summon any God, whether or not He is solar.

That's a good working definition, but it doesn't really tell us what DDM is. What does it mean to bring a deity into the body of a human being and what are its results? From coven to coven, tradition to tradition, there's a great deal of variety, so let's examine the possibilities.

### Rites of Possession
Roughly speaking, DDM/S is a rite of possession; a deity possesses a human being. So, the first question most people will ask is, "Is it real?" If you accept that Gods are real, then surely They can possess a human

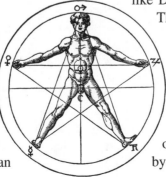

body if They wish to. Is it possible? In Wicca, we learn trance techniques that let us set ordinary consciousness aside, so the question is really the degree to which it's possible: how much consciousness can be set how far aside?

Many religions include possession: Voodoo is perhaps the most famous, but certain Hindu rituals also bring the Goddess into a willing vessel. The Norse tradition of oracular seidh has undergone a modern revival in the last two decades, thanks largely to the work of Diana Paxson. There are others.

### Charge of the Goddess
The widely published Wiccan ritual for DDM goes something like this: The High Priestess stands in "Goddess position" (which looks something like DaVinci's *Vitruvian Man*). The High Priest performs an invocation, reciting while pointing a wand at the High Priestess. The High Priestess then speaks a "Charge." The most common version of the Charge was written by Doreen Valiente, which

begins, "Now listen to the words of the Great Mother, who was of old…" (Some people consider that first paragraph to be part of the invocation, and say the actual Charge of the Goddess begins in the second paragraph, with "Whenever ye have need of any thing, once in the month, and better it be when the moon is full…") It is this structure of DDM that has existed in modern form since at least the 1930s, and arrived in the United States in the early 1960s.

How does reciting a pre-written Charge mesh with being possessed by the actual spirit of a deity? Is it merely play-acting? In Wicca, we believe in immanent deity, meaning the Goddess is already within the High Priestess, even before the invocation is performed. The ritual creates awareness, in the Priestess and in the witnesses, that the Goddess is present; it alters consciousness so that all participants are more receptive to the Goddess's words.

Many is the Priestess who thought she was just play-acting, but found, in the course of DDM, that something more was happening. Words tumbled through her, a presence could be felt. This presence can be exalting and beautiful. For many, it is the entirety of their experience of DDM.

### The Trance Continuum
But the recited Charge is best understood as a safety net. If the *true* possession doesn't occur, the High Priestess has something to do instead of standing there saying "oops, never mind." Indeed, the recitation can complete the process begun by the invocation – she goes into trance. It's also true that not every trance lends itself to words; in the wordless presence of the Goddess, many covens can feel Her touch through the recitation of traditional words, through silence, or through touch.

Trance exists on a continuum. In the movies, you're either *in* or you're not, but in real life, consciousness is constantly being altered in subtle and not-so-subtle ways. The play-acting of possession is an alteration we can call "heightened awareness of Deity." The next step might be called *inspiration* with a presence that the subject can feel in the back of her head, perhaps speaking words, perhaps merely making her trust her own words. As the presence of Deity moves from the back of the head to a side-by-side, shared consciousness, it becomes channeling, and as Deity moves further to the front of the head, or takes over entirely, it graduates into possession. None of these have clear, sharp boundaries; an experienced channel knows that any trance can slip and slide between these states.

### Dangers of Drawing Down the Moon
While some people are naturals at receiving a deity, others can learn the skill. Training to Draw Down involves training the mind in numerous

things: generalized trance states, trust, self-knowledge, shielding, opening, and more.

The big secret here is that Drawing Down isn't actually difficult, but it is dangerous.

Drawing Down itself has hazards. If the circle is not properly protected, the body and mind of the Priestess, being open to the Goddess, become an enticing target for entities other than deities (or entities disguised as deities) to come invited or not. Public rituals are particularly difficult spaces to shield and ward, and chaotic entities can make their presence known – not everything or everyone that can enter your body during a trance state is to your benefit! In addition, participants who don't behave respectfully in the presence of a deity can create another kind of havoc.

The bigger danger, though, is to the ego-mind, the personality, and the psyche of the channel. A mind that is well-trained – through meditation, visualization, and the like – can open itself to messages. Once you've mastered divination or other psychic arts, it's a short journey from receiving messages to receiving the personality of another being. However, while the skill set is similar for making such things happen, the demands on the individual are vastly greater in Drawing Down and other possession work.

## Demons from the Id

While most people are afraid of being fooled, the greater danger is self-deception. Once you begin to believe, uncritically, that the Gods speak through you, problems can occur. Unhealthy ego-inflation is the most obvious: self-importance, throwing your weight around, making others treat you like you're godlike outside of a ritual context – these behaviors will alienate others, but they will also damage you. Worse yet are "demons from the id," to quote a classic science fiction movie. If you haven't done enough work on yourself, if you have no experience in disciplines like psychotherapy, dream journeying or active imagination, you can easily mistake the promptings of your own subconscious mind for the sacred Presence being invoked. Shadow parts of the personality can take over, and devastating damage may result.

Lack of grounding is another problem. Failing to ground thoroughly once in a while is not unusual, but a person receiving the Moon must not only ground before the invocation, she must be grounded in general, with a good connection to her root chakra acting as a lifeline. She must, in other words, have a reliable ability to return to Earth-reality again and again. Many of us have seen occult people suddenly become flaky and unreliable, perhaps even nonsensical. Did they attempt deep trance from an ungrounded state? Once is discomfiting; but monthly, over time, is serious and can break apart one's life.

### A Goddess in Your Body

This kind of trance can be addictive and the ungrounded person is particularly at risk for getting hooked. Practicing deep trance only in a group setting, and only in guarded, ritual space, can protect you from going back for more and more, to the detriment of your daily life.

Low self-esteem can, in some ways, be as bad as ego-inflation. If you are a person who feels small and unworthy, and then you receive a goddess in your body, and experience being worshiped in that form, the dissonance between the ritual self and who you "know" yourself to be can be agony. It can even cause your self-esteem problems to worsen, as the worship ritual serves to heighten the contrasting self-hatred to an unbearable degree.

### Benefits of Drawing Down the Moon

The many potential problems are a good reason for the inexperienced beginner to stay away from DDM. On the other hand, its benefits are profound.

In a ritual setting, with a trained, skilled Priest and Priestess present, Wiccans have the privilege of being in the presence of their Gods. The exaltation, beauty, and raw reality of the experience are truly transcendent. Moreover, the living presence of the Gods keeps our path vital. There are many religions in which the God or Gods spoke to people once, long ago, or in mythic time. It is easy for such a religion to become calcified. Perhaps people become obsessed with doctrine and dogma when it is as close as their religion allows them to get to Deity. When you have a regular opportunity to be in the presence of deities – perhaps even to hear their words – the details become less important. It is for this gift that we take the risks, that we undergo the training, and that we open ourselves to the depth of sacred experience.

– DEBORAH LIPP

*Deborah has been involved in Wicca for thirty years as a High Priestess, teacher and speaker. Be sure to see our book reviewer's impression of Deborah's new book,* The Elements of Ritual *on page 136 of this issue.*

Otto Eckmann

# TALISMAN OF THE MOON

## *Solomon's Sixth Pentacle of the Moon*

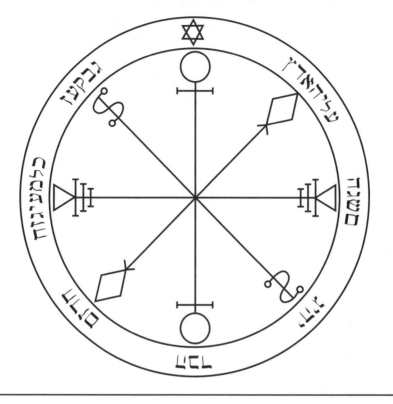

THE SIXTH Pentacle of the Moon should be engraved, drawn, or written in the day and hour of the moon. One of its many uses is to bring rain when it is most needed, as well as allowing the magician to engage the spirits of the moon for change and for astral travel.

When properly used it is said that the Sixth Pentacle of the Moon can bring its user rain and water that will nourish the body and the fields. In this usage it is common practice to engrave it on a piece of silver, which is then placed under water. As long as the pentacle remained submerged in water, the rains will reputedly continue to fall.

The Sixth Pentacle of the Moon can also be used for communion with the spirits of the moon and to seek answers to the unknown from them. During the hour of the moon at night, when the moon is waxing (or better still, full) the user should draw the pentacle on parchment in silver ink. Again, in an hour of the moon, when it is waxing, the magician should hang the sigil from his neck. The magician should draw the Circle of Arte and proceed to invoke to come forth. When the presence is thick, the magician should seek their answer, using direct words of interrogation.

– FRATER P.I.E.V.

# The Hare

IN MANY mystical traditions, the hare is credited with everything from being a trickster to creating the world. You can see the hare in the southern sky, just south of Orion, as the constellation Lepus, as well as in the face of the full moon.

The Uncle Remus Br'er Rabbit stories are based on the African folklore of Hare, his tales showing how the hare relies on his wits to get out of sticky situations, rather than strength or force. In a Bushmen legend, Hare, as the messenger of the Moon, changed a message where the Moon promised that all people would rise again after they die, as the Moon does. But since Hare changed the message, humans do not rise again, and instead are mortal. This frustrated the Moon, who struck Hare across the lip, giving Hare his split lip.

In Native American folklore, the hare is also a trickster, magician, and co-creator of the world. As Nanabozho, he is the founder of the Grand Medicine Society, which consists of shaman/ medicine men in the New England, Great Lakes, and Maritime areas of North America.

### Love, Libido, and Longevity
In China, the hare is the fourth animal in the zodiac, governing Mao (Cancer), as well as the direction of the East, and is a symbol of longevity. People born under this sign are considered to be cunning, strong-willed, and well mannered.

Greek myth considers hares symbolic of love and libido and thus sacred to Aphrodite and attributed to Eros. Hares were also depicted on vases and friezes as prizes to youths competing in athletic competitions.

In Europe and Asia, there is a symbol called "The Three Hares" which depicts three hares, running in a circle. In the center, three ears form a triangle, each connecting to two of the hares. This symbol was found along the Silk Road, in cave paintings, and has connections with Buddhism, Christianity, and Islam.

– HERMES ADRASTOS

# Diana, the Giants, and the Legendary History of England

THE FIRST MAN to print books in England was William Caxton, a cultured merchant and diplomat who died in the 1490s. It was thanks to him that generations of Englishmen were reared on stories of King Arthur and his knights, for it was Caxton who printed the first edition of Sir Thomas Mallory's *Le Mort d'Arthur* [The Death of Arthur] in 1485 from a manuscript now lost. It was a large and heavy volume, priced beyond the means of most readers. But readers in the market for knightly tales and legends of bygone times could also purchase another book from Caxton's press, a smaller volume written in a simpler, livelier style. Its title was *The Chronicles of England*. Here were tales not only of King Arthur, but also of many of the kings before him, like King Bladud, the great necromancer, who used his magic to put up the great stone buildings at Bath, or King Lear and his three daughters. Here, too, is an extensive account of the life and deeds of Merlin, from his childhood onward.

All these ancient kings were successors of the legendary first king of the island that much later came to be called England. The first king of them all was a noble Trojan named Brute (or Brutus), and it was from his name that the island was called Britain. However, the earliest name of that island was not Britain, but Albion. Thereby hangs a tale of Pagan Gods, ancient demons and fabled giants.

The tale, as the chronicler tells it, begins in the far-off East. There was a mighty king in Syria, named Diocletian. He had thirty-three daughters, and his eldest daughter was named Albyne. At a great feast he married all his daughters to thirty-three kings. But his daughters scorned their royal husbands as kings of lesser rank than their father. Urged on by the eldest daughter, each sister cut the throat of her royal husband on the same night. Diocletian wished to burn his daughters alive for their deed, but his councilors urged a lesser punishment, exile from the land. So the daughters went into a well provisioned ship and sailed away forever. At sea, they prayed to their God, whose name was Apollyn, and he guided the ship to an island where no people lived. Albyne named this island Albion, from her own name.

As time passed, so the tale runs, the thirty-three women lusted after men, but there were no men anywhere in the island. Their lust was satisfied by willing demons. The offspring of these women and their demon lovers were horrible giants: Gogmagog, Laugherigan, and many others. They dwelled in caves and hills, and they remained alive long after their human mothers had died.

Now Aeneas had fled Troy after its destruction by the Greeks, and settled in another land. There he sired a son, Brute, whose mother died in childbirth. By accident, Brute later slew his father while they were hunting. As a parricide, Brute, too, was exiled from the land forever. He and his followers took ship. They came to a deserted island in the Mediterranean Sea, where there was an ancient, abandoned city with a temple

to the Goddess Diana and a statue of Her. Brute prayed for guidance before Her statue, as the chronicler records, in these very words:

*Diana, noble Goddess, Lady that all things hast in might and in Thy power – winds, waters, woods, fields, and all things of the world, and all manner of beasts that therein be – to You I make my prayer that Ye me counsel and tell where and in what place I shall have a convenable dwelling for me and for my people. And there I shall make in honor of You a well fair temple and a noble, wherein Ye shall evermore be honored.*

Diana answered him and told him where to find the island called Albion, formerly inhabited by giants, which was destined for him and his people.

It all happened as Diana had foretold. After various adventures they found the island and made land at Totnes, on the river Dart. Brute assembled his people "to make a solemn sacrifice and a great feast in honor and reverence of Diana the Goddess." This was the very first worship offered to any Deity anywhere in England, so far as any chronicle knows. (Much later stories tell how two stones from Brute's very first altar to Diana can still be seen and touched.

One is the Brutus Stone in Totnes, the other is the famous London Stone.)

Soon after this feast, the few giants who remained in the land found Brute and his people and attacked them. In this combat, all the giants were slain, except the mightiest of them, Gogmagog. Brute took Gogmagog prisoner, saving the giant for a wrestling contest with Brute's mightiest warrior, Coryn. Coryn won the contest, though with difficulty, and he cast Gogmagog down from a cliff upon a sharp rock, where he "broke all to pieces and so he died." That place, so the chronicler says, is still called Gogmagog's Leap. Brute rewarded Coryn by giving him the part of the island that is still called Cornwall.

Readers of an earlier number of this *Almanac* (for 2008/9) will remember the Watchers. They were angels who, in the days of the Patriarch Jared, left their heavenly station because they lusted after the daughters of men. To these women they taught magic and the other secret arts, and they sired children on them. These children were the very first giants. The tale of the giants whom Brute found in England, begotten on Albyne and her sisters by demonic lovers, owes something to this ancient lore about the Watchers.

– Robert Mathiesen

# Mirror, Mirror...

*Reflections on myth and magic*

HUMANS are among a select group of animals capable of recognizing their own reflections. Most animals, when confronted with their image in a mirror, react as though another animal is just beyond the glass: they run and cower or scratch and yowl at the newly manifested imposter. Humans, on the other hand, will sit transfixed, preening and pouting at their perfect double. We not only recognize ourselves in the mirror but we ascribe great significance to the power of the mirror's gaze. Mirrors have the power to transfix us, to terrify us, and to offer us a glimpse into other realms.

### Seven Years Bad Luck

Mirrors have long held supernatural significance in a variety of cultures. One of the most commonly held beliefs is that the reflection which appears in

the mirror is actually the gazer's soul. Vampires do not show up in mirrors because they are soulless creatures. If one's image in the mirror appears distorted in any way it is taken as a sign of a corrupt or troubled soul. Damaging a mirror is really damaging ones soul – which explains why breaking a mirror is considered tremendous bad luck (if you happen to break a mirror and wish to avoid the associated seven years bad luck, try submerging the pieces in a south-running stream or grinding the pieces into powder).

There are a variety of other ways in which a mirror can act as a conduit of bad luck. For example, seeing your reflection in a mirror that belongs to someone else might give that person power to influence your actions; infants younger than one year should not be allowed to look at mirrors for fear their soul could become lost in the reflection; if someone dies in the presence of uncovered mirrors, their soul may accidently cross over into the mirror instead of the next life.

## Into the Looking Glass

Mirrors are also considered portals to other realms. Narcissus was pulled into the underworld when he became unable to look away from his own reflection in a still pond. In Jewish folklore, every mirror is an opening to the demon Lilith's cave, where she mates with all manner of beast and births a multitude of monstrous offspring. Vain young girls who stare at their own reflections for too long can be sucked through the mirror into Lilith's cave, never to return. Those who stare too long at their own reflec- 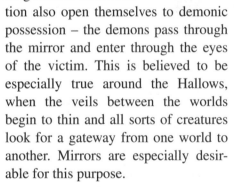 tion also open themselves to demonic possession – the demons pass through the mirror and enter through the eyes of the victim. This is believed to be especially true around the Hallows, when the veils between the worlds begin to thin and all sorts of creatures look for a gateway from one world to another. Mirrors are especially desirable for this purpose.

## Matrimony and Mirrors

Mirrors are not all bad luck and trapped souls, mind you – there are many positive associations with mirrors as well. Anyone wishing to glimpse the face of their true love should sleep with a mirror under their pillow: at night, they will dream of their future husband's or wife's face. It is also supposed that anyone who sees their true love for the first time through the reflection of a mirror is destined for a lifetime of happiness.

## Black Mirrors

Mirrors also bestow the power to look into the future. The Black Mirror is a divination technique heavily influenced by the moon, visions being most clearly defined at the full moon. The original black mirrors were highly polished pieces of obsidian stone, but nowadays any piece of glass with a black backing will do nicely. The technique requires the practitioner to clear their minds and stare deeply through the mirror, focusing on a central point somewhere behind the surface. As the mind clears the mirror will begin to fill with visions of the future. At first, all the diviner will see will be clouds. As the diviner's skill progresses, clearer visions will emerge from the fog.

Whether opening a window to the soul, a gateway to other dimensions, or a glimpse of the future, mirrors are powerful supernatural objects. Next time you find yourself staring at your reflection, try to remember what might be lurking beyond – maybe our animal compatriots see something we don't, after all.

– SHANNON MARKS

# THE PROPER TOPPER

*Top hats – from upscale to stage magic and steampunk*

ADORNING the head may be a subtle way of hinting that, rather than an empty noggin, a great brain ticks within. Ever since the first primitive body wrappings first evolved into fashion, headgear has made powerful statements about one's status in society. Top hats rank among the most symbolic of head coverings.

In the late 1700's, top hats first began to replace the tricorn, when the French artist Charles Vernet portrayed a handsome young man wearing one. An etching shows the Lord Mayor of London wearing a similar hat. The idea attracted British hatter George Dunnage, who, in 1793, began offering silk top hats for sale in his shop. Soon dandies – young trend setters – adopted the topper.

### Abe Lincoln, Uncle Penny Bags, and Queen Victoria's Husband

Within a decade, top hats were popular with both men and women from all walks of life and all around the world – from royals to equestrians to policemen, postmen, farmers and chimney sweeps to officers in the Russian Imperial Army. When Britain's Prince Albert, Queen Victoria's husband, appeared wearing a top hat, its rise to respectability was meteoric. Abe Lincoln's signature stove pipe hat, a variation of the top hat, added to his famous height and presence, perhaps enabling him to win the presidency.

By World War I, although bowlers and ball caps had become everyday wear, top hats continued to evoke formal elegance, wealth, and power. They are a prominent feature of political caricatures, most notably of Uncle Sam. John F. Kennedy and Lyndon B. Johnson wore top hats at their respective inaugurations. Uncle Penny Bags, the rich relative in the game Monopoly, always has his top hat.

### Conjuration and Steampunk

Alice in Wonderland's Mad Hatter as well as stage magicians Auguste Comte and John Henry Anderson created the classical link between magic and top hats. Comte is credited with devising the trick of pulling a white rabbit from his shiny black topper. Twenty-first century magicians continue to don the traditional top hat, a symbol of their command of the mysterious and inexplicable.

The top hat is currently a unique symbol of Steampunk, a movement which, over the past ten years, has mushroomed from an obscure literary genre into an entire subculture. In some ways, Steampunk has been around for over a century; however, the actual term was coined in the 1980's when writer, K.W. Jeter humorously used it to describe futuristic stories set in the Victorian era.

Steampunk is where Victoriana meets science fiction. Mad inventor-scientists create airships, mechanical elephants, and steam powered clocks or pianos in a magical world of ghosts and adventure set against a 19th century backdrop. Recent film versions of Sherlock Holmes and the writings of Jules Verne and H.G. Wells exemplify Steampunk.

### Majestic Techno Explosions

"Steam" – as those in the know call it – builds upon an aesthetic neo-vintage time period, which offers an alternate history. Steampunk is an idealized world. Its growing appeal lies in its diversity. Some who embrace Steam merely enjoy the Victorian ambience. Others are drawn to the Industrial Revolution's majestic technological explosion. The evolution and expansion of Steam is comparable to the growth of Renaissance fairs, Native American Pow Wows, and Civil War reenactments.

In addition to top hats, other significant symbols of Steam include aviator goggles, corsets, gloves, and spats. Splashes of color are allowed, but Steampunk is mostly a world of black, white, brown and grey, suggesting the 19th Century reality of factory smoke stacks and train stations. Observers are unsure of exactly where Steam's future direction lies, but it's definitely gathering momentum, especially among the young and creative. A Steampunk baby contest was featured not long ago on the CBS Sunday Morning program. The winner's curls were adorned by her tiny black top hat worn at a jaunty angle.

–MARINA BRYONY

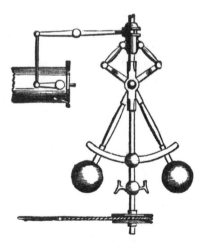

23

# Hathor

*Mistress of inebriety without end*

AUDACIOUS, LUSTY, and confident, Hathor is the mother of many Egyptian gods and goddesses. She has had more temples built in her honor than any other Egyptian goddess. Among the few Egyptian goddesses not to have suffered a tragedy or loss, Hathor epitomizes self-confidence and pleasure. She is most familiar in her guise as a cow goddess, sporting a bovine headdress. However, many are less familiar with Hathor's important roles as a goddess of fertility, eroticism, death, music and dance. Egyptians, male and female alike, celebrated her by dancing in her honor. Even kings have danced for Hathor!

Hathor is a goddess with a dual nature: although typically a nurturing, loving goddess, she also simultaneously possesses a "take no prisoners" side. Hathor can be a deity of extremes. When enraged, she transforms into Sekmet, fierce and bloodthirsty. A famous myth describes how Sekmet ran amuck through the countryside, only finally calming down when she was given a drink of beer that had been dyed red. In her drunken state, she mistook it for blood and drank herself into an inebriated stupor, in the process transforming back into even-tempered Hathor. The people of Egypt celebrated her return by getting intoxicated along with her – Hathor loves a party!

## All Acts of Love and Pleasure are my Rituals

To embody Hathor is to embrace the feminine to the fullest: the well-worn phrase *All Acts of Love and Pleasure are my Rituals* can be said of Hathor.

She dances, she loves to display her body, and she enjoys her sexuality. Nothing can defeat her. There are no well-known stories of any adversity affecting Hathor. Even when exhibiting her bellicose side, she readily turns into a cheerful drunk. She epitomizes beauty and defines sensuality. Hathor is called the Lady of Myrrh, the fragrance of that rare resin is said to signal her presence. She is specifically associated with the use of myrrh as a perfume. Many

consider Hathor to be the patron of cosmetic artists and perfumers.

Her dances are sensual and erotic. Hathor herself danced nude or semi-nude in front of her father, the sun god, Ra, to make him laugh. She is the goddess of sexual-expression in the form of dance. Many relate her dances to masturbation for both sexes. Today's erotic/ exotic dancers can look to Hathor as a patron, for Hathor sought to give pleasure to all.

## Seven Hathors

Hathor is best loved as a guardian and protector of women. She is the Lady of Birth and Death, said to be at the side of all mothers during childbirth, appearing in the form of the Seven Hathors. These Seven confer and announce the fate – including the date and manner of death – of every child. Hathor also reputedly appears on the Other Side, following death, to receive souls and guide them to Osiris, Lord of Death. It is no small wonder that Hathor is among Egypt's most beloved deities.

Hathor's many titles include Lady of Stars, Golden One, Mistress of Heaven, Mother of Mothers, Mistress of Life, Lady of the Vulva and Lady of the West. She is a sky goddess and a tree deity, as well. Usually depicted as a woman with a crown of bovine horns, she can also appear as a woman with the head or ears of a cow. The Greeks identified Hathor with Aphrodite, while the Romans associated her with Venus. Many myths surround her origin, with some as contradictory as Hathor's own nature appears to be. Benevolent, kind and nurturing, yet also potentially bloodthirsty, Hathor will let nothing get in the way of her pleasure.

– SUSAN ASSELIN

# MOON GARDENING

## BY PHASE

*Sow, transplant, bud and graft*     *Plow, cultivate, weed and reap*

     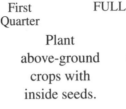     

| NEW | First Quarter | FULL | Last Quarter | NEW |
|-----|-----|-----|-----|-----|
| Plant above-ground crops with outside seeds, flowering annuals. | Plant above-ground crops with inside seeds. | Plant root crops, bulbs, biennials, perennials. | | Do not plant. |

## BY PLACE IN THE ZODIAC

### Fruitful Signs

Cancer – Most favorable planting time for all leafy crops bearing fruit above ground. Prune to encourage growth in Cancer.

Scorpio – Second only to Cancer, a Scorpion Moon promises good germination and swift growth. In Scorpio, prune for bud development.

Pisces – Planting in the last of the Watery Triad is especially effective for root growth.

Taurus – The best time to plant root crops is when the Moon is in the sign of the Bull.

Capricorn – The Earthy Goat Moon promotes the growth of rhizomes, bulbs, roots, tubers and stalks. Prune now to strengthen branches.

Libra – Airy Libra may be the least beneficial of the Fruitful Signs, but is excellent for planting flowers and vines.

### Barren Signs

Leo – Foremost of the Barren Signs, the Lion Moon is the best time to effectively destroy weeds and pests. Cultivate and till the soil.

Gemini – Harvest in the Airy Twins; gather herbs and roots. Reap when the Moon is in a sign of Air or Fire to assure best storage.

Virgo – Plow, cultivate, and control weeds and pests when the moon is in Virgo.

Sagittarius – Plow and cultivate the soil or harvest under the Archer Moon. Prune now to discourage growth.

Aquarius – This dry sign of Air is perfect for ground cultivation, reaping crops, gathering roots and herbs. It is a good time to destroy weeds and pests.

Aries – Cultivate, weed, and prune to lessen growth. Gather herbs and roots for storage.

*Consult our Moon Calendar pages for phase and place in the zodiac circle. The Moon remains in a sign for about two-and-a-half days. Match your gardening activity to the day that follows the Moon's entry into that zodiac sign.*

# The *MOON* Calendar

is divided into zodiac signs rather than the more familiar Gregorian calendar.

**2013**

**2014**

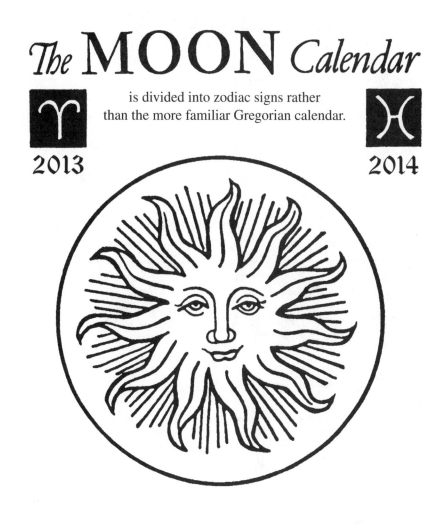

Bear in mind that new projects should be initiated when the Moon is waxing (from dark to full). When the Moon is on the wane (from full to dark), it is a time for storing energy and the wise person waits.

Please note that Moons are listed by day of entry into each sign. Quarters are marked, but as rising and setting times vary from one region to another, it is advisable to check your local newspaper, library or planetarium.

*The Moon's Place is computed for Eastern Standard Time.*

# The Frogs Desiring a King

THE FROGS were living as happy as could be in a marshy swamp that just suited them; they went splashing about caring for nobody and nobody troubling with them. But some of them thought that this was not right, that they should have a king and a proper constitution, so they determined to send up a petition to Jove to give them what they wanted. "Mighty Jove," they cried, "send unto us a king that will rule over us and keep us in order." Jove laughed at their croaking, and threw down into the swamp a huge log, which came splashing down into the swamp. The frogs were frightened out of their lives by the commotion. All rushed to the bank to look at the horrible monster. After a time, seeing that it did not move, one or two of the boldest of them ventured out towards the log, and even dared to touch it. Still it did not move. Then the greatest hero of the frogs jumped upon the log and commenced dancing up and down upon it, whereupon all the frogs came and did the same. Then for some time after, the frogs went about their daily business without taking slightest notice of their new King Log, lying in their midst. This did not suit them, so they sent another petition to Jove, saying "We want a real king; one that will really rule over us." Now this made Jove angry and so he sent a big stork that soon set to work gobbling the frogs all up. Then the frogs repented, but it was too late.

Moral: Better no rule than cruel rule.

# capricorn
## December 21 – January 19
*Cardinal Sign of Earth ▽ Ruled by Saturn ♄*

| S | M | T | W | T | F | S |
|---|---|---|---|---|---|---|
| **SATURN** *Etherial father, mighty Titan, hear, great fire of Gods and men, whom all revere: Endu'd with various council, pure and strong, to whom perfection and decrease belong.* (continued below) | | | | | **DEC. 21** Winter Solstice ❄ Aries | **22** Plan a new life |
| **23** Gather personal strength Taurus | **24** | **25** Carlos Casteneda born, 1925 Gemini | **26** Bide your time | **27** Pray to the moon | **28** Wolf Moon Cancer | **29** WANING |
| **30** Leo | **31** Consult an oracle | **JAN. 1** 2013 | **2** Buy a coconut Virgo | **3** | **4** Libra | **5** Stress lessens |
| **6** Dismiss doubt Scorpio | **7** | **8** Sagittarius | **9** Feast of Janus | **10** Brew a strong tea Capricorn | **11** | **12** WAXING Aquarius |
| **13** | **14** Toss a coin three times Pisces | **15** | **16** Carry bloodstone Aries | **17** Robert Fludd born, 1637 | **18** | **19** Don't be stubborn Taurus |

*Consum'd by thee all forms that hourly die, by thee restor'd, their former place supply... No parts peculiar can thy pow'r enclose, diffus'd thro' all, from which the world arose, O, best of beings, of a subtle mind, propitious hear to holy pray'rs inclin'd; The sacred rites benevolent attend, and grant a blameless life, a blessed end.* – Orphic Hymn to Saturn

# Athena turns spiders into living shuttles

ATHENA was both the goddess of war and goddess of the arts. She delighted in weaving and provided the Olympians with shimmering garments, their colors exquisite beyond description. Athena was astounded to learn that Arachne, a peasant girl, declared her own work to be superior. Athena descended and arranged a contest. Looms were set up and piles of wondrous fabrics evolved, all colors of the rainbow, shot through with silver and gold threads, unmatched for silkiness and elegant designs. Finished at the same moment, Arachne's weaving was in no way inferior. Anger the goddess of war at your peril... Athena beat Arachne's head with a shuttle. The girl crept away, disgraced and humiliated, and hanged herself. But repentance crept into Athena's heart. She removed the noose, sprinkled Arachne with a magic potion, and the girl morphed into a spider. The weaver and others of her kind are classified as *Arachnida*. What geometric wonders they conceive and weave!

– Barbara Stacy

# aquarius

## January 20 – February 18

*Fixed Sign of Air ♒︎ Ruled by Uranus ♅*

| S | M | T | W | T | F | S |
|---|---|---|---|---|---|---|
| Jan. 20 | 21 | 22 | 23 Raise a storm | 24 | 25 Gather in a circle | 26 Storm Moon |
| | Gemini | | | Cancer | | Leo |
| 27 WANING | 28 | 29 Johann Reuchlin born, 1455 Virgo | 30 Prepare for the Sabbat | 31 Oimelc Eve Libra | Feb. 1 Candlemas | 2 Light a red candle Scorpio |
| 3 ◐ | 4 Light a white candle | 5 Honor Oya Sagittarius | 6 | 7 Capricorn | 8 Evangeline Adams born, 1868 | 9 Fortune smiles Aquarius |
| 10 Year of the Snake | 11 WAXING Pisces | 12 | 13 Act with caution Aries | 14 | 15 Lupercalia Taurus | 16 Live, laugh, love |
| 17 ◑ | 18 Speak freely Gemini | | | | | |

## URANUS

Great Heav'n, whose mighty frame no respite knows, father of all, from whom the world arose: Hear, bounteous parent, source and end of all, forever whirling round this earthly ball; Abode of Gods, whose guardian pow'r surrounds th' eternal World with ever during bounds; Whose ample bosom and encircling folds the dire necessity of nature holds. Ætherial, earthly, whose all-various frame azure and full of forms, no power can tame. All-seeing Heav'n, progenitor of Time, forever blessed, deity sublime, Propitious on a novel mystic shine, and crown his wishes with a life divine. – Orphic Hymn to Uranus

## YEAR OF THE WATER SNAKE
*February 10, 2013 – January 29, 2014*

Year 4711

ACCORDING to legend, Buddha rewarded twelve animals by granting them stewardship over a year, thus creating the East Asian zodiac. Snake is the sixth of these twelve animals. Five elements (fire, water, metal, earth, and wood) further distinguish the animals. Every sixty years, the pattern of element-animal pairs repeats. This is the Year of the Water Snake. Expect a subtle interplay of emotions to motivate people and impact situations. Remember, snakes charmed people long before we charmed them. Creation myths from Native American, Hindu, African, and Celtic traditions, not to mention the biblical tale of Adam and Eve, all feature spiritual and divine snakes. The Water Snake, immersed in the liquid of life, promises to be transformative. Its fangs may poison old patterns, ultimately allowing new cosmic eggs to hatch and give birth to the future.

Those born in a Year of the Snake are elegant, charismatic, mysterious, charming, and wise. Marvelous storytellers possessing a sense of humor, they are charitable, fashionable dreamers who appreciate stability.

Years of the Snake
1917, 1929, 1941, 1953, 1965, 1977, 1989, 2001, 2013

*Chinese New Year commences with the second new moon after the winter solstice. It begins in late January to mid-February. If you were born in a Year of the Snake, uncoil and slither forward proudly to cast your serpentine spell. It's your season. Savor a wish fulfilled, enjoy rewards, and cultivate promising opportunities. More information on the Water Snake can be found on our website at http://The WitchesAlmanac.com/AlmanacExtras/.*

*Illustration by Ogmios MacMerlin*

| S | M | T | W | T | F | S |
|---|---|---|---|---|---|---|
| | | Feb. 19 | 20 Exercise caution Cancer | 21 | 22 Love with all your being | 23 Leo |
| 24 Look for a mermaid tomorrow | 25 Chaste Moon Virgo | 26 WANING | 27 Consider an alternative Libra | 28 Moina Mathers born, 1865 | March 1 Matronalia | 2 Scorpio |
| 3 | 4 Sagittarius | 5 Trust an omen | 6 Be specific Capricorn | 7 | 8 Aquarius | 9 Teach sorcery |
| 10 Daylight Savings Time begins @ 2am Pisces | 11 | 12 WAXING Aries | 13 Use hypnosis | 14 Algernon Blackwood born, 1869 | 15 Taurus | 16 Eat something sweet |
| 17 Read poetry Gemini | 18 Minerva's Day ⇨ | 19 | 20 Cancer | | | |

## NEPTUNE

*Hear, Neptune, ruler of the sea profound, whose liquid grasp begirts the solid ground... Thy awful hand the brazen trident bears, and ocean's utmost bound, thy will reveres: Thee I invoke, whose steeds the foam divide, from whose dark locks the briny waters glide; Whose voice loud founding thro' the roaring deep, drives all its billows, in a raging heap; When fiercely riding thro' the boiling sea, thy hoarse command the trembling waves obey.* – Orphic Hymn to Neptune

# Spring

Now every field is clothed with grass, and every tree with leaves; now the woods put forth their blossoms, and the year assumes its gay attire.

—VIRGIL

# aries

## March 20 – April 19

*Cardinal Sign of Fire △ Ruled by Mars ♂*

| S | M | T | W | T | F | S |
|---|---|---|---|---|---|---|
| **TO THE NEW MOON** <br><br> *Greeting to you, New Moon, kindly jewel of guidance! / I bend my knees to you, I offer you my love. / I bend my (continued below)* | | | Mar. **20** <br> 2012 <br> Vernal <br> Equinox <br> Cancer | **21** | **22** <br> *Hold your temper* <br> Leo | **23** |
| **24** <br> *Clyde Barrow born, 1909* <br> Virgo | **25** <br> *Bond with your familiar* | **26** <br> ⚪ | **27** <br> *Seed Moon* <br> Libra | **28** <br> WANING | **29** <br><br> Scorpio | **30** <br> *Bide your time* |
| **31** <br> *Beware of fire* <br> Sagittarius | April **1** <br> All Fools' Day | **2** <br><br> Capricorn | **3** <br> ◑ | **4** <br><br> Aquarius | **5** <br> *Let luck rule* | **6** <br><br> Pisces |
| **7** <br> *Clean a gemstone* | **8** | **9** <br> *Consult a candle flame* <br> Aries | **10** <br> ⚫ | **11** <br> WAXING <br> Taurus | **12** <br> *Wake up your garden* | **13** <br><br> Gemini |
| **14** <br> *Honor creativity* | **15** | **16** <br> *Charles Chaplin born, 1889* <br> Cancer | **17** <br> *Take a chance* | **18** <br> ◑ | **19** <br><br> Leo | |

*knees to you, I raise up my hands to you, / I lift up my eyes to you, New Moon of the Seasons. / Greeting to you, New Moon, darling of my love! / Greeting to you, New Moon, darling of graces, / You journey on your course, you steer the flood tides, / You light up your face for us, New Moon of the Seasons.* — excerpt from *Moon Lore*

# HAWTHORN

## *Uath*

THE HAWTHORN is a small tree, seldom exceeding fifteen feet in height. Its long thorns provide protection against storm and grazing animals for larger trees like oak and ash that grow up beneath it and eventually supplant it. It also affords thorny shelter for birds and other wildlife that feast on its scarlet autumn berries. Although it grows well in most soils, the hawthorn prefers damp sandy earth for germination and is often a bird-sown tree. The bark is dark grey-brown and splits into a pattern of random squares with

age. The flowers grow in clusters of white or palest pink and exude a strong unusual scent.

Hawthorn is so strongly associated with the Celtic May Eve festival that "may" is a folk name for it. Whitethorn is another name popular in Brittany, where the tree marks fairy trysting places. Sacred hawthorns guard wishing wells in Ireland, where shreds of clothing are hung on the thorns to symbolize a wish made. The Roman goddess Cardea, mistress of Janus who was keeper of the doors, had as her principal protective emblem a bough of hawthorn. "Her power is to open what is shut; to shut what is open."

Thorn trees are bewitched, according to old legends, and the hawthorn in particular caught the imagination of all Western Europe from earliest recorded time. In some cultures it served as a protection against lightning; in others it was thought to have purifying power. It was deemed the tree of chastity by Old Irish. Greek brides wore crowns of hawthorn blossoms in May, but Romans considered the month of May an inappropriate time to wed and the flowering hawthorn an ill omen, especially if brought inside the home. To the Turks, the hawthorn signified erotic desire. Mother Goose, in whose name so much of our folklore literature is preserved, yields a beauty secret:

*The fair maid who, the first of May,*
*Goes to the fields at break of day,*
*And washes in dew from the*
*  hawthorn tree,*
*Will ever after handsome be.*

# taurus

## April 20 – May 20

*Fixed Sign of Earth ▽ Ruled by Venus ♀*

| S | M | T | W | T | F | S |
|---|---|---|---|---|---|---|

**ASTARTE**
Ancient Egyptians often symbolized their deities in the form of animals, but the earliest representation of the divine figure in the company of animals belongs to the Phoenician earth (continued below)

APRIL **20**

| S | M | T | W | T | F | S |
|---|---|---|---|---|---|---|
| 21 <br><br> Virgo | 22 <br> *Yehudi Menuhin born, 1916* | 23 <br><br> Libra | 24 <br> Partial lunar eclipse ⇨ <br> *Plant seeds* | 25 <br> (Hare Moon) <br> Scorpio | 26 <br> WANING | 27 <br><br> Sagittarius |
| 28 | 29 <br><br> Capricorn | 30 <br> Walpurgis Night | MAY 1 <br> Beltane | 2 <br> ◐ <br> Aquarius | 3 | 4 <br> *Cast flowers into a garden* <br> Pisces |
| 5 <br> *Befriend a black dog* | 6 <br><br> Aries | 7 | 8 <br> White Lotus Day <br> Taurus | 9 <br> ● | 10 <br> Partial solar ⇦ eclipse | 11 <br> WAXING <br> Gemini |
| 12 | 13 <br><br> Cancer | 14 | 15 <br> *Speak a secret word* | 16 <br> *Liberace born, 1919* <br> Leo | 17 | 18 <br> ◑ |
| 19 <br><br> Virgo | 20 <br> *Cast the runes* | goddess Astarte. Those rare humans gifted with the ability to communicate with wild creatures have probably existed since time began... One thousand years later, Astarte's earthly qualities would merge with those of the Greek Moon goddess Artemis, for both were addressed as **"The Lady of Wild things."** – excerpt from *Moon Lore* | | | | |

*Apollo, God of Poetry and Music, and Hermes, God of Eloquence,
from Moretus'* Philomathi Musea Iuveniles, *Antwerp, 1654.*

# gemini

## May 21 – June 20

*Mutable Sign of Air △ Ruled by Mercury ☿*

| S | M | T | W | T | F | S |
|---|---|---|---|---|---|---|
| | | MAY 21 Libra | 22 | 23 Scorpio | 24 Partial lunar eclipse ⇨ Vesak Day ⇨ | 25 Dyad Moon Sagittarius |
| 26 WANING | 27 Dashiel Hammett born, 1894 Capricorn | 28 | 29 Oak Apple Day Aquarius | 30 | 31 Pisces | JUNE 1 |
| 2 Aries | 3 Observe the clouds | 4 Taurus | 5 Night of the Watchers | 6 | 7 Tell a secret Gemini | 8 |
| 9 WAXING | 10 Cancer | 11 | 12 Pursue your whims Leo | 13 Basil Rathbone born, 1892 | 14 Virgo | 15 Enjoy solitude |
| 16 | 17 Listen to the birds Libra | 18 | 19 Scorpio | 20 | CYNTHIA | |

**CYNTHIA**

A name for the Moon goddess that was derived from Mount Cynthos on Delos, the birthplace of Artemis and Apollo. Leto, a beautiful maiden made pregnant by the sky god Zeus… she was denied refuge everywhere for all feared the wrath of Hera, wife of Zeus, who was enraged by his infidelity. Leto was finally granted sanctuary on the desolate isle of Delos where Artemis was safely delivered. Artemis… then assisted her mother at the birth of her twin brother. The myth provides another role for the Moon goddess – patroness of women in childbirth.     – excerpt from *Moon Lore*

# TAROT'S MOON

XVIII

THE MOON.

THERE IS A THIN LINE between genius and madness. The moon sits firmly on this line. In one guise, the moon is a muse, prompting artists and laymen alike to create with reckless abandon. But one must be careful not to indulge these lunacies too fully, for creativity taken to its most extreme is destruction. Will this new phase of artistic energy find you akin to the crab, who crawls from primordial ignorance and sets out on the path to illumination, or will the wolf in you win out, letting loose primal urges kept dormant by convention?

The Moon card denotes a crossroads, a choice, or a turning point. Habits and old signifiers hang in the balance, ready to be rejuvenated or torn down to make room for what lies ahead. Whichever path you choose to pursue, remember: the Moon travels in darkness, but its presence foretells the Sun.

# cancer
## June 21 – July 22
*Cardinal Sign of Water ▽ Ruled by Moon ☽*

| S | M | T | W | T | F | S |
|---|---|---|---|---|---|---|
| **THE RITE**<br>*To renew psychic energy, increase divinatory perception and to nourish the soul: At the full Moon closest to summer solstice and when the Moon is high, go to an (continued below)* | | | | | JUNE 21<br>Summer Solstice ☼<br>Sagittarius | 22<br>*Draw down the moon* |
| 23<br>(Mead Moon)<br>Capricorn | 24<br>Midsummer<br>WANING | 25<br>*Gather St. Johnswort* ⇐<br>Aquarius | 26 | 27<br><br>Pisces | 28 | 29<br>*Peter Paul Rubens born, 1577*<br>Aries |
| 30 | JULY 1<br>*Avoid turmoil* | 2<br><br>Taurus | 3 | 4<br>*A carefree day*<br>Gemini | 5 | 6<br>*Hang a silver ornament* |
| 7<br><br>Cancer | 8 | 9<br>WAXING<br>Leo | 10<br>*Cast a spell* | 11 | 12<br>*Find the crescent moon*<br>Virgo | 13<br>*Collect a fallen feather* |
| 14<br><br>Libra | 15 | 16<br><br>Scorpio | 17<br>*Phyllis Diller born, 1917* | 18<br><br>Sagittarius | 19 | 20<br><br>Capricorn |
| 21<br>*Pray to the moon* | 22<br>(Buck Moon)<br>Aquarius | *open space carrying a small bowl of fresh spring water. Position yourself so as to capture the Moon's reflection in the bowl. Hold it as steadily as you can in both hands for a slow and silent count to nine. Close your eyes and while holding the image of the Moon in your mind, drink the water to the last drop.* — excerpt from Moon Lore | | | | |

# Why Sunflowers Came to the World

THE GODDESS MARI inhabited the Basque mountains when the world was still in darkness. The deity worked magic of highest art. Inside caves, Mari made herself comfortable as a snake or a bat. On the outside, she assumed the appearance of a celestially beautiful woman. But Mari's grandeur was lost to her mortal sons and daughters in their deep obscurity.

The Basques lived in eternal fear of the dragons, flying bulls and other evil spirits that arose from the bad place underground. Corpses piled high and finally the people asked Mari for protection.

The goddess created a bright being called Moon. A luminous crescent appeared in the sky. The first glimpse of light! Terrified, the villagers ran home and hid in haylofts and under beds. But curiosity got the better of them; they peeked out and emerged. Soon the inhabitants enjoyed roaming the moonlit mountains. In time the moon grew bigger until it hung in the sky, a full circle spilling brightness. People suddenly felt dizzy with joy, singing, dancing, whooping, feasting, drinking, falling downhill or in love.

Unfortunately the monsters also chose to wander by moonlight and the attacks increased. Mari's children again pleaded for protection. This time she created the Sun and said, "Now you will have the Sun during the day and the Moon at night."

At first people shielded their eyes against the radiance, but soon rejoiced in the unfamiliar warmth and brilliance. Around them Mari's amazing grace manifested and new life sprang up like a green mantle flung over the earth. As one of the blessings, evil spirits fled to darkness below at the first glimmer of sunrise.

Yet the Basques still longed for safety at night, when monsters continued to threaten. Mari promised to relieve the pestilence – and so she did, with divine ingenuity. The goddess created the *eguskilore* (*eguski*, sun; lore, flower), the thistle that bears the ring of golden rays, protective mark of Sun. In doorways and gardens the stalk looms high, the bloom thrusts forward like a neighbor across the fence settling in for a good gossip. Sunflowers cheer the heart of mortals. And Mari's magic always serves to perfection. The flowers protect by their resemblance to what monsters fear most – the light of day. Since the Basque region was blessed with sunflowers, dragons and their nasty ilk have rarely, rarely been sighted.

– BARBARA STACY
*adapted from a Basque folk tale*

# leo

## July 23 – August 22

*Fixed Sign of Fire △ Ruled by Sun ☉*

| S | M | T | W | T | F | S |
|---|---|---|---|---|---|---|
| | | JULY 23 WANING Ancient Egyptian New Year | 24 Speak to Isis | 25 Pisces | 26 Stanley Kubrick born, 1928 | 27 Aries |
| 28 | 29 Taurus | 30 | 31 Lughnassad Eve Gemini | AUGUST 1 Lammas | 2 | 3 Cancer |
| 4 | 5 Marvel at the midnight sea | 6 Leo | 7 WAXING | 8 Do not haggle Virgo | 9 Bless the bees | 10 Libra |
| 11 | 12 | 13 Diana's Day Scorpio | 14 | 15 Sagittarius | 16 Julie Newmar born, 1935 | 17 Capricorn |
| 18 | 19 Sing at midnight Aquarius | 20 Wort Moon | 21 WANING Pisces | 22 | | |

## ðIAΝA

*Originally the name of an Italian wood deity who became identified with the Greek Artemis, and like her, symbolized the Moon. The Romans celebrated Diana's Day on August 13th and it was the custom to choose a particularly fine tree and decorate it with her emblems: the crescent, bow and arrows, silver masks, tiny animal figures... A common gesture of respect used to address Diana in both town and country observances was with the fingers of the right hand clenched and pressed hard against the forehead.* — excerpt from *Moon Lore*

# Fruit and Nuts

Lamon, the gardener, to Priapos prays,
Grant that his limbs keep strong and all his trees,
And this sweet gift of fruit before him lays:
This golden pomegranate, this apple, these
Elfin-faced figs, new grapes, a walnut green
Within its skin, cucumbers' leafy sheen,
And dusky olives, gold with gleaming oil –
To you, oh friend of travelers, this spoil

*– Palatine Anthology*

# virgo

## August 23 – September 21

*Mutable Sign of Earth* ♍ *Ruled by Mercury* ☿

| S | M | T | W | T | F | S |
|---|---|---|---|---|---|---|
| | **ARTEMIS** "She who hunts the clouds," is the original personification of the Moon, akin to the night luminary as her twin brother, Apollo, (continued below) | | | | AUG. 23 Aries | 24 |
| 25 Walk in the woodlands Taurus | 26 | 27 Best is yet to come | 28 Gemini | 29 John Locke born, 1632 | 30 Cancer | 31 Watch the tide change |
| SEPT. 1 | 2 Praise the worthy Leo | 3 Memphis Slim born, 1915 | 4 Virgo | 5 | 6 WAXING | 7 Listen to the birds Libra |
| 8 | 9 Ganesh Festival Scorpio | 10 Consult the tarot | 11 Sagittarius | 12 | 13 Capricorn | 14 |
| 15 Aquarius | 16 Carry luck in your pocket | 17 Pisces | 18 Tsukimi ⇨ | 19 Barley Moon | 20 WANING Aries | 21 |

is to the Sun. The Greeks conceived the character of the Moon goddess in image and nature to be an ideal woman – a being worthy of worship. Describing her as virgin and huntress implied far more than mere sexual innocence and the pursuit of game. In classical Greek, the word "virgin" had a deeper meaning. It signified self-possession, dignity and compassion – purity as it related to spiritual integrity.

— excerpt from *Moon Lore*

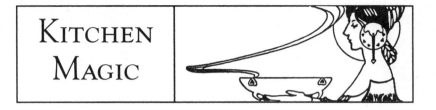

# Pistachio

*Lovers in the orchard*

THE PISTACHIO is a powerful aphrodisiac, inspiring great passion of all kinds in those who consume the plump green jewels. The pistachio is so alluring and irresistible that the Queen of Sheba declared all pistachios grown within her kingdom to be property of the court. Young lovers seeking confirmation of their happy future together need look no further than an orchard of pistachio trees. If, in the silence of midnight, the lovers hear the audible POP! of pistachio seeds cracking open as they ripen above, then so too will their love ripen. Originally grown in the cool, dry climate of ancient Persia, it wasn't long before the cultivation and consumption of pistachios spread throughout the Middle East and eventually to Europe and Asia. Today, pistachios are also grown in California and continue to inspire great passion.

### Pistachio Butter: A simple way to enjoy the richness of pistachios

In a food processer, combine one cup shelled pistachios with about a quarter cup warm water (use a bit less or a bit more, depending on desired consistency). Add a pinch of salt and sweeten to taste with honey or simple syrup. (To make simple syrup: add one part sugar to one part water and heat until the sugar is dissolved

– SHANNON MARKS

*Try our recipe for a pistachio-laden sweet Greek treat when you visit our Almanac extras page at http://The WitchesAlmanac.com/AlmanacExtras/.*

# libra

### September 22 – October 22
*Cardinal Sign of Air ♎ Ruled by Venus ♀*

LIBRA

| S | M | T | W | T | F | S |
|---|---|---|---|---|---|---|
| SEPT. 22<br>Autumnal Equinox<br>♌<br>Taurus | 23<br>Horned God rules | 24<br>Catch a falling leaf<br>Gemini | 25 | 26<br>◑<br>Cancer | 27<br>Cyril Scott born, 1879 | 28 |
| 29<br><br>Leo | 30 | OCT. 1<br>Bonnie Parker born, 1910<br>Virgo | 2<br>Eat an apple | 3 | 4<br>●<br>Libra | 5<br>WAXING |
| 6<br>Count the stars<br>Scorpio | 7<br>Stay indoors | 8<br><br>Sagittarius | 9<br>Try something different | 10<br><br>Capricorn | 11<br>◐ | 12<br>Proceed slowly<br>Aquarius |
| 13<br>Gather fall flowers | 14 | 15<br><br>Pisces | 16 | 17<br>Partial lunar eclipse ⇨<br>Aries | 18<br>Blood Moon | 19<br>WANING<br>Taurus |
| 20 | 21<br>Observe the moon glow<br>Gemini | 22 | | | | |

Ediplis · Lunc

## ΤΗΕ SUN AND ΤΗΕ ΜΟΟΝ

*The simple fact that our planet has a single Moon to light the night and one Sun to warm our day has surely led to human conceptions of duality. Forms recognized as male and female, good and evil, certainty and chance, instinct and reason have been dramatized in spiritual thought and the arts from the beginning of recorded time. And through these expressions we understand that all things involve their opposites and ultimately form one whole.* – excerpt from *Moon Lore*

47

Merlin. *Illustration by Aubrey Beardsley*
*Roundel on contents-page verso of*
Le Morte Darthur, *Vol. 1,*
*published by J.M. Dent & Co., London, 1893.*

# scorpio

## October 23 – November 21

*Fixed Sign of Water ▽ Ruled by Pluto ♀*

SCORPIVS

| S | M | T | W | T | F | S |
|---|---|---|---|---|---|---|
| **hecate**<br><br>*The Moon before rising, after setting, and for the three nights when it is lost from sight belong to Hecate.* – excerpt from *Moon Lore* | | | Oct. 23<br><br>*Conjure spirits* | 24<br><br><br>Cancer | 25 | 26<br><br><br>Leo |
| 27 | 28<br><br>*Erasmus born, 1467* | 29<br><br><br>Virgo | 30<br><br>*Talk to the dead* | 31<br><br>*Samhain Eve*<br><br>Libra | Nov. 1<br><br>*Hallowmas* | 2<br><br>*Use no salt*<br><br>Scorpio |
| 3<br><br>**Total Solar Eclipse** | 4<br><br>⇐ *Daylight Savings Time ends @ 2am*<br>Sagittarius | 5<br><br>WAXING | 6<br><br><br>Capricorn | 7<br><br>*Bring offerings to a hilltop* | 8 | 9<br><br><br>Aquarius |
| 10 | 11<br><br>*Carry a charm*<br><br>Pisces | 12<br><br>*Grace Kelly born, 1929* | 13<br><br><br>Aries | 14 | 15<br><br>*Renew psychic energy*<br>Taurus | 16<br><br>*Hecate Night* |
| 17<br><br>Snow Moon | 18<br><br>WANING<br><br>Gemini | 19 | 20<br><br>*Read and rest*<br><br>Cancer | 21 | | |

## TRIVIA

*The word may now be synonymous with worthless knowledge, but in time gone by it was the name Romans gave Hecate. Her triple-form statues stood where three roads met and so they called her Trivia – tri, three and via, road. The crossroads, sacred to the dark goddess, suggest moments of decision.* – excerpt from *Moon Lore*

# Cats in Islam

AN ORAL TRADITION tells of the Prophet Muhammad's fondness for cats. One day, as the Prophet began to dress for afternoon prayers, he came upon his favorite cat, Muezza, sleeping soundly on the sleeve of his robe. Rather than disturb the feline's sound slumber, Muhammad cut the sleeve off his robe and proceeded to prayer. When he returned, Muezza bowed to him in thanks for his kindness. Muhammad stroked Muezza's fur three times, granting the cat the ability to always land on its feet.

Since then, cats have held a special place in Islamic tradition. Cats are considered very clean animals: water consumed by a cat is considered safe for people to share. While all animals are deserving of protection and compassion, cats are especially revered: it is forbidden for cats to be sold or traded for goods and anyone who abuses a cat will be punished with torture for eternity.

An Islamic household keeping a cat as a pet must follow certain rules. The cat must be provided plenty of clean water and wholesome food as well as being allowed the freedom to roam unrestricted. The rewards for treating cats can be great: one story tells of a Sufi Shaykh who, upon arriving in Paradise, was asked by Allah if he knew why he was allowed into Paradise. The Shaykh recited the devotions he undertook on a daily basis, his good deeds, the many people he taught – but none of these fine actions was what allowed the Shaykh into Paradise. Finally, Allah revealed that what opened the gates of Paradise to the Shaykh was a simple act of kindness to a helpless kitten. On a bitterly cold night, the Shaykh spotted the poor kitten shivering on the street. He picked it up and tucked it in his coat, saving the kitten's life and guaranteeing his own salvation.

– TENEBROUS RAE

# sagittarius

## November 22 – December 20

*Mutable Sign of Fire △ Ruled by Jupiter ♃*

| S | M | T | W | T | F | S |
|---|---|---|---|---|---|---|
| **TAROT MOON** *Out of the Gothic darkness and of unknown origin, the Tarot cards of divination appeared. Partial sets from the two oldest decks exist today – one painted for a mad French king in 1392, the other* (continued below) | | | | | Nov. 22 | 23 Leo |
| 24 | 25 ◑ Virgo | 26 | 27 *Try again* | 28 Libra | 29 | 30 *Brownie McGhee born, 1915* Scorpio |
| Dec. 1 *Light a midnight fire* | 2 ● Sagittarius | 3 WAXING | 4 *Try even harder* Capricorn | 5 *Otto Preminger born, 1906* | 6 *Trust a friend* Aquarius | 7 |
| 8 Pisces | 9 ◐ | 10 *Hold on to your power* Aries | 11 | 12 | 13 *Sing by candlelight* Taurus | 14 *Practice meditation* |
| 15 *Indulge* Gemini | 16 *Fairy Queen Eve* | 17 ○ Oak Moon | 18 *Saturnalia* ⇦ WANING Cancer | 19 | 20 *Take revenge* Leo | |

*commissioned by a wealthy 15th century Milanese family. The first printed cards were probably produced a century or so later. The classic Tarot of Marseilles is a series of crude archaic woodcuts, images of surprising power. The Marseilles Moon card is particularly rich in symbolism. Small wonder that the appearance of this trump in a reading is greeted with a shiver. The standard interpretation is one of illusion, deceit, darkness, and terror.* — excerpt from Moon Lore

*Tell me about Pan... with his goat's feet and two horns... Through wooded glades he wanders with dancing nymphs who foot it on some sheer cliff's edge, calling upon Pan, the shepherd-god, long-haired, unkempt... Often he courses through the glistening high mountains, and often on the shouldered hills, he speeds along slaying wild beasts, this keen-eyed god.* — HOMERIC HYMN TO PAN

## Pan's Invitation

"I WANT you to want me. I want you to forget right and wrong; to be as happy as the beasts, as careless as the flowers and the birds. To live to the depths of your nature as well as to the heights. Truly there are stars in the heights and they will be a garland for your forehead. But the depths are equal to the heights. Wondrous deep are the depths, very fertile is the lowest deep. There are stars there also, brighter than the stars on high. The name of the heights is Wisdom and the name of the depths is Love. How shall they come together and be fruitful if you do not plunge deeply and fearlessly? Wisdom is the spirit and the wings of the spirit, Love is the shaggy beast that goes down. Gallantly he lives, below thought, beyond Wisdom, to rise again as high above these as he had first descended. Wisdom is righteous and clean, but Love is unclean and holy. I sing of the beast and the descent: the great unclean purging itself in fire: the thought that is not born in the measure or the ice or the head, but in the feet and the hot blood and the pulse of fury. The Crown of Life is not lodged in the sun: the wise gods have buried it deeply where the thoughtful will not find it, nor the good: but the Gay Ones, the Adventurous Ones, the Careless Plungers, they will bring it to the wise and astonish them. All things are seen in the light – How shall we value that which is easy to see? But the precious things which are hidden, they will be more precious for our search: they will be beautiful with our sorrow: they will be noble because of our desire for them. Come away with me, Shepherd Girl, through the fields, and we will be careless and happy, and we will leave thought to find us when it can, for that is the duty of thought, and it is more anxious to discover us than we are to be found."

*– from* The Crock of Gold *by James Stephens, Macmillan, 1912: Originally published in the 1975/1976 Witches' Almanac.*

# capricorn
## December 21 – January 19
*Cardinal Sign of Earth ♉ Ruled by Saturn ♄*

| S | M | T | W | T | F | S |
|---|---|---|---|---|---|---|
| 🌙 **WAXING** — *As the Moon increases, its form takes the shape of the capital letter D: D for Daring… a time for creativity, expansion, and development… Later on as darkness falls, it shines like a beacon of hope, raising your spirits and assuring the success of your ventures.* – Moon Lore | | | | | | Dec. **21** Winter Solstice ❄ |
| **22** Gather holly | **23** Virgo | **24** The wheel turns | **25** 🌓 Libra | **26** | **27** Johannes Kepler born, 1571 Scorpio | **28** |
| **29** Sagittarius | **30** | **31** Touch a pine tree Capricorn | Jan. **1** 2014 | **2** WAXING Aquarius | **3** Wish upon the moon | **4** Jacob Grimm born, 1785 Pisces |
| **5** | **6** Don't tempt fate Aries | **7** 🌗 | **8** Gather snow | **9** Feast of Janus Taurus | **10** Gift a talisman | **11** Gemini |
| **12** A chill | **13** | **14** Fly by night Cancer | **15** 🌕 Wolf Moon | **16** WANING Leo | **17** | **18** Make a sacrifice |
| **19** Virgo | **WANING** — *Rising later night after night, the Moon diminishes in size, now assuming the form of the letter C: C for Caring. The time has come to relax, restore energy, and quietly dispel negative influences in your life. Banish fear as the Moon wanes.* – excerpt from *Moon Lore* 🌙 | | | | | |

53

# The Ballad of the White Horse

Before the gods that made the gods
Had seen their sunrise pass,
The White Horse of the White Horse Vale
Was cut out of the grass.

Before the gods that made the gods
Had drunk at dawn their fill,
The White Horse of the White Horse Vale
Was hoary on the hill.

Age beyond age on British land,
Æons on æons gone,
Was peace and war in western hills,
And the White Horse looked on.

For the White Horse knew England
When there was none to know;
He saw the first oar break or bend,
He saw heaven fall and the world end,
O God, how long ago!

*– excerpt of "The Vision of the King"*
*from* The Ballad of the White Horse
*by GK Chesterton*

# aquarius
## January 20 – February 18
*Fixed Sign of Air ♎ Ruled by Uranus ♅*

| S | M | T | W | T | F | S |
|---|---|---|---|---|---|---|
| | Jan. 20 | 21<br><br>May<br>evil recede<br><br>Libra | 22 | 23 | 24<br><br><br><br>Scorpio | 25<br><br>Love<br>passionately |
| 26<br><br>Burn<br>old habits<br><br>Sagittarius | 27 | 28<br><br>Alan Alda<br>born, 1688<br><br>Capricorn | 29<br><br>Wish on<br>the<br>new moon | 30<br><br><br><br>Aquarius | 31<br><br>WAXING<br>Year of<br>the Horse | Feb. 1<br><br>Oimelc Eve<br><br>Pisces |
| 2<br><br>Candlemas | 3<br><br>Treat<br>your<br>familiar<br>Aries | 4 | 5<br><br>Open<br>a new<br>door<br>Taurus | 6 | 7<br><br>Embrace<br>change<br><br>Gemini | 8 |
| 9 | 10<br><br>Prepare<br>moon<br>candles<br>Cancer | 11 | 12<br><br>Abraham<br>Lincoln<br>born, 1809<br>Leo | 13 | 14<br><br>Storm<br>Moon | 15<br><br>Lupercalia<br><br>WANING<br>Virgo |
| 16<br><br>Embrace<br>love | 17<br><br>Sign no<br>documents<br><br>Libra | 18<br><br>Ring<br>bells | | | | |

## MOON PASSAGE

Once long ago humans depended upon the Moon for reckoning time, planting crops and harvesting the sea... In a sense the lovely silver sphere... is more mysterious now despite the exploration of its surface. The Moon's curious forces continue to exert their influence over us and our planet. We and the oceans of Earth still unceasingly respond to the Moon's magnetic appeal. As a symbol of mystic significance, appreciated by so many ancient religious expressions, the Moon remains as potent as ever, at least to the poet, the artist and the witch. – excerpt from *Moon Lore*

# Amazon River Dolphins

THE RIVER people believe that pink dolphins (the *botos*) used to be humans many, many years ago, and that they can turn back into humans whenever they want. When they turn back into humans, they kidnap young boys and girls and take them to live with them in their underwater villages and cities.

It is also believed that dolphins can use water creatures as objects for their daily lives, besides using them for food. The walking catfish become their shoes, the anacondas are their hammocks, the sting rays are their hats, and the water snakes are their belts.

When a person is taken into the dolphin's world of the dark Amazon waters, he or she is immediately transformed into a dolphin. If this happens, this person will never come back to be a human again.

This might be a way for the people in the Amazon to explain when someone drowns in the river or becomes lost in the forest.

Dolphins are at the top of the food chain in the Amazon River basin along with the jaguars, harpy eagles, anacondas and caimans. All of these animals – except dolphins – are hunted for food or for their skins. Even though there are laws protecting all these animals, dolphins probably aren't hunted because the myths and superstitions help protect them. People don't kill dolphins because they think it's very bad luck to kill them. They don't eat them because they believe dolphins used to be people.

– BÉDER CHÁVEZ
*Stories from the River*

# pisces

## February 19 – March 20
### Mutable Sign of Water ∇ Ruled by Neptune ♆

| S | M | T | W | T | F | S |
|---|---|---|---|---|---|---|
| **SELENE**<br>...Selene persuades Zeus to grant her beloved one wish. Endymion chooses perpetual youth by means (continued below) | | | FEB. **19** | **20**<br><br>Scorpio | **21** | **22**<br><br>Sagittarius |
| **23**<br>Wear the color of the sun | **24**<br>Winslow Homer born, 1836<br>Capricorn | **25** | **26**<br><br>Aquarius | **27**<br>Assemble at the crossroads | **28**<br>Matronalia ⇨<br>Pisces | MARCH **1** |
| **2**<br>WAXING<br>Aries | **3**<br>Search early memories | **4**<br><br>Taurus | **5**<br>Decorate a tree | **6** | **7**<br><br>Gemini | **8** |
| **9**<br>Daylight Savings Time begins @ 2am<br>Cancer | **10**<br>Bathe in blue water | **11** | **12**<br>Vaslav Nijinsky born, 1890<br>Leo | **13** | **14**<br><br>Virgo | **15**<br>Assemble at the 13th hour |
| **16**<br>Chaste Moon | **17**<br>WANING<br>Libra | **18**<br>Unlucky day | **19**<br>Minerva's Day<br>Scorpio | **20** | | |

of perpetual sleep, and retires to a deep underground cave. In another, it is Selene who imposes everlasting sleep on her handsome lover. Whichever, Endymion must have been aroused on occasion, as all sources agree that he fathered fifty daughters with the goddess. And when the Moon wanes, it is said that Selene visits her lover deep in his cavern of repose.      – excerpt from Moon Lore

# Alphecca

*The crown jewel of the scorpion*

LONG AGO, when horoscopes were first cast, the ancient astrologers gazed into the heavens and followed cosmic motion with sand clocks. The celestial bodies were grouped in categories. First came the luminaries, the bright lights of the sun and moon. Next came the stars. Thousands of them sparkled, seemingly motionless, in the nighttime sky. They were called the fixed stars. After a very long time, stargazers realized that this was a misnomer. The stars do move against the backdrop of deep space, but ever so slowly. Spanning a century, the distance they travel is barely perceptible. Their variations in distance, in light-years from Earth, and chemical composition give the stars variable colors and magnitude or brightness. Interpreted astrologically, each star emits unique cosmic energies, often these are fortunate and glorious, but sometimes sinister and truly evil.

Alphecca is a brilliant white star of the second magnitude. It has impressed astrologers since at least the time of Ptolemy. Its frequency attunes to Mercury, Venus, and Mars. Poetic speech, literary ability, artistry, dignity, leadership, wealth, sorrow, and scandal through children and loneliness are all keynotes of Alphecca's influence. Called the "jewel in the crown of the Scorpion," currently it's located at about 12 degrees of Scorpio. Alphecca's name comes from the Arabic and means "the bright one of the broken ring." It also has a Latin name, *Gnosia gemma stella coronae*, translating "gem, star of the crown of Knossos."

Alphecca is one of the legendary fifteen Behenian (root) stars assigned magical attributes in medieval ritual magical traditions by Heinrich Cornelias Agrippa, (chapters 47 and 52, Book Two of Agrippa's *Three Books of Occult Philosophy*). It can be invoked to protect virtue, grant revelations through dreams, or attract friendship and honor. The juice of the herb rosemary, mixed with equal parts of clover and ivy, as well as the gem topaz (a birth stone of Scorpio) were used magically to court Alphecca's favor.

When a fixed star conjoins a luminary or planet it can dominate an event or an individual's destiny. Here are some keynotes for precisely how Alphecca can be significant. Consider only the conjunction when placing a fixed star in a birth chart and use an orb of just three degrees.

Alphecca's influence is quite prominent during the year ahead. It will be conjoined by both the sun and moon at the rare total solar hybrid eclipse on November 6, 2013. Magical rituals focused on Alphecca during the eclipse might yield immediate and dramatic results. Saturn will conjoin Alphecca early in the spring and again from September 23 – November 21, 2013. During those times, spells invoking Alphecca can assist with developing good rapport between those of different generations.

– DIKKI-JO MULLEN

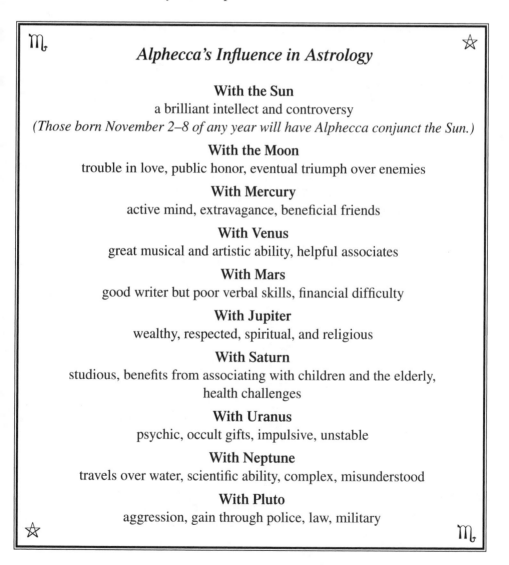

## Alphecca's Influence in Astrology

**With the Sun**
a brilliant intellect and controversy
*(Those born November 2–8 of any year will have Alphecca conjunct the Sun.)*

**With the Moon**
trouble in love, public honor, eventual triumph over enemies

**With Mercury**
active mind, extravagance, beneficial friends

**With Venus**
great musical and artistic ability, helpful associates

**With Mars**
good writer but poor verbal skills, financial difficulty

**With Jupiter**
wealthy, respected, spiritual, and religious

**With Saturn**
studious, benefits from associating with children and the elderly,
health challenges

**With Uranus**
psychic, occult gifts, impulsive, unstable

**With Neptune**
travels over water, scientific ability, complex, misunderstood

**With Pluto**
aggression, gain through police, law, military

# What the Moon Sees

## Moonshine and moon-cursers

COUNTLESS POEMS, stories, and songs recount what we see when we look at the full-moon sky. Dark clouds scud across the fully illuminated disk, lending a silver cast to the fields and forests below. Telescopes and satellites send back crisp images of this mysterious celestial body. Fine art and primitive scratchings alike, deriving from cultures all over our planet, show the moon in her great glory. But what about the moon herself? What does the moon see? The moon sees many things, including things of an illicit nature.

### Moonshine

Take moonshine, for example. No, not the rays of reflected light from our beloved orb's surface, but the alcoholic liquid that has been concentrated through the process of distillation. In the Appalachians and other regions of the colonial United States, making whisky from surplus grain was an accepted cottage industry. Mountain folk made a mash of corn meal or fruit, fermented it, and then distilled it into a strong liquor to earn extra money from grain that they could not otherwise sell. Sold outright for cash, it was also traded for things they couldn't grow on the farm: bolts of cloth, sugar, and gunpowder.

Some was kept aside for personal use, and not just as a recreational drug. The strong alcohol was used as a topical antiseptic for wounds and a painkiller for more severe injuries. In more skilled hands, it was used as a solvent for making herbal tinctures from herbs and roots, whose properties the mountain folk had learned from the local Native Americans.

### Whisky Tax

Contrary to popular belief, it was not Prohibition in 1920 that drove the making of hard liquor into the shadows, but the introduction of an excise tax on whisky in 1791. Many resented the tax, and not just for economic reasons. The United States government was only a mere fifteen years old and some questioned the right of the government to impose such a tax.

Those who continued to produce whisky without paying taxes did so in secret, deep in the woods at night, using only moon light for illumination. Though enforcement of the tax – like the moon – waxed and waned over the years, the distillation continued in secret, beneath that moon light, endowing the spirit with one of the names that we know it by today – moonshine.

 Moonshiners weren't beyond exaggerating tales of "haints" to keep government revenue agents ("revenooers") and potential thieves away. Were angry ghosts really wandering the mist-filled hollows? Only the moon knows for sure.

### Moon-Cursers

The name "moon curser" or "moon cusser" was applied to two different occupations in the eighteenth century.

In the days before street lights in London, one type of moon-curser was more commonly known as a link-boy. These young lads earned their living by carrying a lit torch to light the way for pedestrians at night. Because their services were not needed at the full moon, they were said to curse the moon for the loss of their wages.

The more nefarious type of moon-curser was the torch-bearer who only pretended to guide people safely home, but instead guided them to a dark alley where robbers lay in wait. Similarly, pirates used torches to wreck ships that they would then plunder. The captain of a ship looking for safe harbor would see the torchlight of the pirates in a lonely cove. Thinking it was illumination from a lighthouse, the crew would steer toward it, into the rocks where the looters lay in wait. Those rogues who laid the trap cursed the full light of the moon, for it prevented them from carrying out their ruse.

–Morven Westfield

# The Moon and the Weather

Pale Moon doth rain, red Moon doth blow,
white Moon doth neither rain nor snow.

Clear moon, frost soon.

A dark mist over the Moon is a promise of rain.

The full Moon eats the clouds away.

A new Moon and a windy night
sweep the cobwebs out of sight.

A red Moon is a sure sign of high winds.

Blunt horns on a crescent Moon
presage a long spell of fair weather.

A single ring around the Moon that
quickly vanishes heralds fine weather.

When the new Moon holds the old Moon in its arms
(ring around the new Moon) disasters at sea occur.

Sharp horns on the sickle Moon indicate strong winds.

And should the Moon wear
a halo of red, a tempest is nigh.

*– excerpt from* MOON LORE

# Window on the Weather

EARTH'S CLIMATE, with all its perceived extremes, is really the manifestation of nature's ability to balance and vanquish momentary excesses of heat and cold. These extremes are the product of the cyclical nature of seasons and planetary progressions that influence the fluctuations of solar radiation coming into contact with Earth's varying material composition, texture, and color. This varies our planet's heat budget; in turn creating weather, which is nature's mechanism to disperse these inequities and fosters conditions allowing life to flourish. Indeed, in its normal state, our climate is not static, but instead demonstrates cycles that ebb and flow over millions of years. No doubt, whatever paradigm now exists regarding our perception of what will arrive will change many times over, as the seasons unfold. This is the nature of the uncertain universe and the exciting weather adventures that we will all soon enjoy. The following is an educated estimate of what the short-term outlook will bring.

— TOM C. LANG

# SPRING

MARCH 2013. On average, March brings the greatest monthly rise in temperatures of any month, a trend that often creates great turbulence. Southern storms carry great moisture and the potential for severe weather for southern states. Several East Coast storms can cause flooding from the Appalachians to New England and heavy wet snow falls in the higher peaks. From the Carolinas to Florida, isolated tornadoes are possible, with the greatest risk in Central Florida, Northern Alabama, and Georgia. Farther west, the long-term drought begins to ease in Texas and Oklahoma, improving prospects for abundant winter wheat. The Rockies enjoy quiet weather, whereas these are stormy times in the Pacific Northwest.

APRIL 2013. The Northeast enjoys an early spring after a mild winter. Lake ice has melted by about the tenth, as temperatures rise. Spring flowers bloom early from New York to Virginia. Sporadic rough weather shifts west to the Ohio Valley, with several tornado threats during the late afternoons and evenings. A late season wet snowfall can be expected in the Northern Plains, with welcome rainfall in the Plains and as far west as Colorado. Late season skiing is good in Colorado, Montana, and Utah. On the West Coast, winds are occasionally strong from land-falling Pacific storms that last about twelve hours. Tides are especially high during the full moon, with any onshore winds.

MAY 2013. Fine spring weather covers the entire East Coast, with normal rainfall aiding gardeners. The risk of frost ends for most of the country, except in valley locations near the Canadian border and in the Northern Rockies. With generally quiet weather, a fine growing season is underway throughout the heartland. In Texas and Oklahoma, the peak of the tornado season arrives, along with the risk of hail. Daily temperatures exceed 80 degrees in Florida, Arizona, and Southern California, yet humidity remains moderate. As Pacific storms end, the West Coast enjoys sunny and pleasant weather. Meanwhile, great differences in temperature are felt in New England, between immediate coastal communities and those just a few miles inland and away from chilly afternoon sea breezes, fog, and mist.

## SUMMER

JUNE 2013. Few weather extremes are likely to be felt across the country, as the solstice arrives. In the Southeast, early summer heat is quelled by frequent rains, the effects of the recent El Nino that will keep temperatures cool. Occasional rainy days are interspersed with spells of sunshine from the Mid-Atlantic to New England. The Great Lake States enjoy fine June weather with ideal growing conditions. The threat of frost ends and the Great Plains are lush and green, with abundant spring rains. In the West, June weather brings consistent temperatures and fresh Pacific breezes. In Florida, brush fires are less common than usual.

JULY 2013. Summer heat is less intense than usual. Several cold fronts bring afternoon thunderstorms to the Northeast and Midwest. A brief tornado may be spawned in Central New England and Upstate New York. Afternoon thunderstorms arrive on Florida's West Coast, bringing dazzling lightning to Tampa and Fort Myers. Heat and humidity build across the Plains, with afternoon showers common from Minnesota to the Dakotas, where severe thunderstorms will keep farmers alert. Monsoonal showers bring afternoon rain to the Continental Divide, although the weather is mainly dry. The West is generally sunny and pleasant.

AUGUST 2013. Remnants of a weak El Nino episode in the Pacific Ocean brings a slow start to the beginning of the tropical cyclone season. Only an occasional flare-up is likely, with the far eastern Atlantic seeing its first hurricane by mid month – one that will likely stay far from land. Rain will fall with less frequency in the Southeast, while New England remains relatively cool for the season. Occasional rain falls from Maine through Vermont. Early harvest conditions build across the heartland with good drying conditions prevalent. Texas heat is not as intense as in recent years and rainfall is more abundant. A rare summer rainfall may occur in southern California. Chicago should be on alert for a tornado.

## AUTUMN

SEPTEMBER 2013. Hurricane activity will reach peak intensity by about the 10th. While a land-falling storm with major consequences is unlikely, East Coast residents should remain wary throughout the month and develop a family hurricane plan. Summer temperatures linger in the South, with afternoon thunderstorms becoming less frequent in Florida. Conditions remain dry nationwide, with excellent harvest conditions in the heartland. Balmy Pacific breezes are pleasant in coastal California, Oregon, and Washington. Sunshine is prevalent, with a fine spell of summer weather throughout the East.

OCTOBER 2013. Crisp nights and pleasant days quicken the pace of fall weather across the north. Dry weather prevails in most places, although a dusting of snow in the Rockies provides a fine background for colorful foliage. Vestiges of El Nino keep the storm track to the south, bringing sporadic rains to the Mississippi and Southern Ohio Valleys. Dry weather, with a hint of frost arrives in New England, as the growing season ends. Brush fires are problematic in Florida and Southern California. The first Pacific storms arrive in the Pacific Northwest, with brief gales in Seattle and Portland, Oregon. The Midwest is cool and dry and Texas enjoys drought relief, brought by tropical rains from a disturbance in the Gulf of Mexico.

NOVEMBER 2013. Colder air sweeps through the northern Rockies and into the Plains, accompanied by gusty winds and showers of rain changing to snow, but with little accumulation. The advance of the cold is initially intermittent, lasting only a day or so. While temperatures are seasonable in the Northeast, a brief dusting of snow is possible from Upstate New York to Central New England, where a white Thanksgiving is possible. The Mid-Atlantic becomes somewhat stormy, with windswept rains occurring several times. Meanwhile, an outbreak of severe weather threatens the Southeast. The first lake effect snows of the season fall in Michigan. Minneapolis temperatures fall to near zero by the 30th.

## WINTER

DECEMBER 2013. Snowfall is widespread, falling from the Northern Plains to New England. The heaviest threat occurs throughout interior sections of the Northeast, with potentially heavy pre-Christmas snowfall. Occasional rainfall sweeps the West Coast, together with strong coastal winds and heavy mountain snow, extending east to the Rockies and Central Plains. In Florida, sunny and cool days lead to chilly night time temperatures, with a brief frost possible. The Gulf Coast states enjoy generally pleasant weather, although a coating of ice can develop in northern Louisiana and southern Arkansas.

JANUARY 2014. Icy air covers much of the country and it is colder than most recent winters. Snowfall is heavy in southern New England, with the arrival of several Nor'easters. Travel from Washington to Portland, Maine can be impacted shortly after the 1st. Temperatures far below zero are felt in the Plains and throughout the Great Lakes. Lake effect snows are heavy near Cleveland, east of Chicago, and from Rochester to Syracuse, New York.

Stormy winter weather is also felt on the West Coast, as heavy windswept rains fall, snarling traffic in Los Angeles. High passes are clogged by winter snow. Skiing in the Rockies is excellent this year. Florida enjoys temperatures in the low 70s, with chilly nights.

FEBRUARY 2014. The cold eases somewhat in the East, but occasional snows continue in some places, especially in New England. Snow changes to rain in New York, Philadelphia, and Washington. The snow cover remains deep farther north, providing excellent winter sports conditions. The deepest cold air is centered in the Plains, with numerous mornings bringing below zero readings, early in the month. February is relatively dry there. The West Coast remains stormy, with mudslides threatening southern California. Snow can be seen in the foothills surrounding San Francisco and San Jose. A rare snow falls near Seattle. Bright weather is enjoyed throughout Florida, although central Florida experiences nocturnal tornadoes, causing concern and limited damage.

# The Journey of Destiny: Orí

THE Yoruba of southwestern Nigeria have long honored a pantheon of deities (Òrìsà) that often embody many natural phenomena. However, there is one Òrìsà who does not embody a natural energy, but who is singularly each individual's most important Òrìsà. The single most important guiding concept in Ifá and Òrìsà worship is the concept of one's destiny. Each person has a destiny that is embodied in the personal Òrìsà: Orí. It is upon the base of Orí that we build the journey that is this lifetime. Orí must be sought out, understood, and propitiated on a regular basis.

So what is Orí? When talking about Orí, the Yoruba often refer to a complex that is fundamentally important to the life that each lives. Although by inference, Orí would seem to be a singular entity, there are in fact three distinct parts of our inner being that are important as each travels through this life.

## The Inner Constellation

To the Yoruba, the first among the constituent parts of our inner spiritual being that is important is what many understand as destiny. Each person, prior to coming to earth, chose a destiny while kneeling before Olódùmarè. This chosen destiny is called *orí alásìwàyé èdá* and is what most will understand as the Òrìsà Orí. The choice made becomes intimately entwined with and part of the complex of the inner constellation. Each carries this with them in their journey to earth and this more than any being is their guiding energy in life.

The riddle of Orí is that it seems to be a choice, yet, in the same instance, is a deity, an emanation of the high god Olódùmarè and therefore Òrìsà. It is through this paradox that one realizes that so important is a chosen journey that it has been created as an Òrìsà to each individual. In fact, Orí is the single most important Òrìsà in each person's life. It becomes impossible to separate the individual from the choices that they made in heaven, their Orí, and the life that they are living here on earth.

Given the above, the Yoruba understand Orí as Òrìsà. As a matter of fact, every person's Orí is regarded as their own personal Òrìsà who is more interested in his or her own personal affairs and sojourn here on earth than any other Òrìsà. Òrìsà belongs to everyone; Orí belongs only to the individual.

### Choosing the Head

Prior to making the journey to earth, each had to choose a head to go with their *orí alásìwàyé èdá*. The head is referred to simply as orí. This component is also a part of destiny and is the receptacle of Orí (*orí alásìwàyé èdá*.) Some pick a head that is good and some pick a head that is ill-formed. The choice of a head is made at the home of Àjàlá and, like Orí, will remain with the individual throughout his or her entire journey here and, in many ways, will influence success. The choice of a good head will enhance their life while here on earth and, conversely, the choice of a bad head will inhibit.

These first two parts, the inner constellation, are choices that are made. The final component of the spiritual being is the Orí Inú. This is each person's "inner head" or, more properly, their inner being. While destiny and the head are chosen, the Orí Inú is not. This is the part that is carried through incarnations. In order to

truly be successful in life, the Orí Inú must be in alignment with our Orí (sic *orí alásìwàyé èdá*.)

### The Pursuit of Happiness

Many go through life seeking not only success, but also happiness. The pursuit of happiness seems empirical in nature; however, what escapes many is the intimate connection between happiness and destiny. If one understands a good (i.e. happy) destiny as only one filled with abundance and ease, one may indeed fail in understanding the connection between happiness and destiny. It is the journey that becomes important, the fulfilling that becomes the focus, rather than the end. There is no end; there is only the journey. The final end can only be a place among the ancestors.

So, how does one get in touch with Orí? How does one know one's destiny and gain happiness? There are three modes of aligning with Orí that are equally essential to the Yoruba. Firstly, they recognize daily the existence of Orí. Upon waking, their first act of the day is to pray to their Orí and give thanks for the new day. As a matter of course, they will put their hands to their head (again, the receptacle of our Orí) and praise their own destiny/Orí, the singular Òrìsà who will stay by their side throughout their entire journey.

### Praise Prayer and Propitiating the Orí

As well as praising Orí on daily basis, the Yoruba also occasionally propitiate their Orí. This is called Ìborí. The individual who is going to propitiate his or her Orí would bathe and achieve a calm mental state. Preliminarily, he or she would offer a praise prayer to Olódùmarè, his or her Orí, the Irúnmolé, as well as his or her ancestors. After paying homage to the deities, the Orí is told what is being offered to it and Orí Inú is asked to act in concert with destiny. In the propitiating of Orí, offerings are presented to the seat of the Orí (the crown of the head), the Orí Inú (through the navel), and to the Orí of our ancestors (paternally through the big toe of the right foot and maternally through the big toe of our left foot).

As well as praising and propitiating Orí, the individual should seek out the advice of the Ifá oracle. He or she understands that, when consulting the oracle, destiny is, in many ways, simultaneously consulted. The Òrìsà in charge of the oracle, Orùnmìlà, is said to be *elérì ìpín* – witness to all of destiny. Given this, it is understood that Orùnmìlà can guide each as to the wishes of his or her Orí. He can tell them what is satisfying to their destiny.

### Without Good Character, All Comes to Naught

Lastly, the Yoruba believe that you must always act with good character (*ìwà*).

A man can have a good destiny and a good head, but without good character, all will come to naught. To take this a step further, those who have chosen difficult destinies and have not chosen the best of heads can enhance their lot through ìwà. As a matter of fact, it is only by acting with good character and showing generosity to others that one can actualize one's own destiny. While the control of character may seem to be the easiest of all endeavors, many forget to act in such a way. A cool, compassionate, and humble head can carry an individual a long way in life and is the third leg that will allow all to be in alignment with our destiny.

The many instances where Orí is referenced in the corpus of Ifá are certainly worth noting as a reference. In closing, I would like to quote one such ese, which reminds of the importance of Orí, Ògúndá Méjì. In here, we are entreated to how Orùnmìlà demonstrated to each Òrìsà, including himself, that they cannot accompany their devotees to the end of their journeys. In the end it was only Orí who would accompany the individual through the entire journey and it is because of Orí that each receives blessing…

– IFADOYIN SANGOMUYIWA

*Bí mo bá lówó lówó*
*Orí ni n ó rò fún*
*Orí mi, ìwo ni.*
*Bí mo bá bímo láyé*
*Orí ni n ó rò fún*
*Orí mi, ìwo ni.*
*Ire gbogbo tí mo á ni láyé*
*Orí ni n ó rò fún*
*Orí mi, ìwo ni.*
*Orí pèlé*
*Atèté níran*
*Atèté gbe'ni k'òòsà*
*Kò sóssà tí í dá'ni í gbè lèyìn Orí eni*


If I have money,
It is Orí whom I will praise,
My Orí, it is you.
If I have children on earth,
It is Orí whom I will praise,
My Orí, it is you.
All good things that I have on earth,
It is Orí whom I will praise,
My Orí, it is you.
Orí, I salute you
You do not forget (your devotees)
You bless before the other Òrìsà
No Òrìsà blesses
Without the consent of Orí

# The Lunar Nodes

## *Understanding the celestial dragon*

THE MOON'S NODES are sensitive points in space, located where the moon crosses the ecliptic (Earth's orbit). Of great significance in analyzing both natal charts and future events, eclipses occur when a lunation, a new or full moon, is near a lunar node. A solar eclipse occurs with the new moon; a lunar eclipse at the full moon. Stargazers once thought that,  during an eclipse, the sun or moon was swallowed by a gigantic dragon. The head of the dragon was called Caput Draconis and its tail, Cadua Draconis. The moon's north node, noted in the ephemeris, is the dragon's head; the south node is always directly opposite. For example, on March 20, 2013, the north node is 18 degrees Scorpio 03 minutes, so the south node is 18 degrees Taurus 03 minutes.

The north node assures a strengthening influence with the benevolent natures of Venus and Jupiter. The south node is sinister. Akin to Saturn and Neptune, it's draining and confusing. The north node lends elements of luck to the house it occupies, amplifying the positive traits of any planets within 3 degrees. Spiritual astrologers identify the north node with good karma: gifts earned in past lives. The nature of the gift is revealed by the house position and planets nearby. In contrast, the south node shows potential dead ends, which are best avoided.

Dwelling on the south node assures delays and obstacles. The north node brings nourishment. The south node is elimination and release. A traditional reference summarizes the nodes as the dragon's mouth and anus. The north node provides celestial illumination for clear direction, while the south node shines a yellow light for caution. Each horoscope has both. The beauty and wonder of the nodes is that they show how to wrestle with and overcome animal nature through natural gifts and assets.

Contemporary astrologers no longer see the nodes as a monstrous dragon. (Vedic astrologers link the head and tail to two demons, Rahu and Ketu, respectively.) Instead, they are clues to help successfully meet life's challenges by rising above the inner dragons hidden within individual psyches or encoded in the deeper meanings of events.

Lunar nodes are a retrograde cycle, moving backwards to complete a full revolution of the zodiac in a span of 18.6 years.

– DIKKI-JO MULLEN

## Keywords for the Nodes in the Signs and Houses

**Aries – Libra** (1st and 7th houses)
Balance personal will with obligations to others.

**Taurus – Scorpio** (2nd and 8th houses)
Understand true values while fulfilling material needs.

**Gemini – Sagittarius** (3rd and 9th houses)
*(note: the north node is exalted in Sagittarius
and the south node in Gemini)*
Wise communication and selection of studies and travel plans.

**Cancer – Capricorn** (4th and 10th houses)
Family life is balanced with the quest for recognition and success.

**Leo – Aquarius** (5th and 11th houses)
Heartfelt creative expression is balanced with social and
community obligations.

**Virgo – Pisces** (6th and 12th houses)
Routine service balances with reverie and solitude.

✳

## Keywords for Planetary Conjunctions with Nodal Influences

**Sun** – expansion, leadership

**Moon** – sensitivity, heritage

**Mercury** – original thought, mobility

**Venus** – finances and creativity

**Mars** – energy, military service, athletic ability

**Jupiter** – education, standard of living, wealth

**Saturn** – property, responsibilities, generation gap

**Uranus** – reform, originality, technology

**Neptune** – the sixth sense, spirituality, dreams

**Pluto** – ecology, mystery, crime rate

# Merry Meetings

*A candle in the window, a fire on the hearth,*
*a discourse over tea…*

This year *The Witches' Almanac* visits with Peter Grey and Alkistis Dimech of Scarlet Imprint, an independent publishing house specializing in talismanic, esoteric, and occult books. Founded in 2007, Scarlet Imprint is among the leading publishers of the occult world. Their titles include *The Red Goddess*; *Datura: An Anthology of Esoteric Poesis*; and *Pomba Gira and the Quimbanda of Mbumba Nzila*.

---

*Scarlet Imprint has established a potent presence in the field of high quality occult books. Tell us about Scarlet Imprint's mission and how this venture began.*

Scarlet Imprint happened by the hand of fate. We had to publish *The Red Goddess* in a particular talismanic fashion to fulfil a promise Peter made to Her. 156 copies were consecrated and sold by word of mouth under the Scarlet Imprint banner. At the same time we had begun our work with the Goetia together and *Howlings* was born from this. Precious little practitioner material was finding its way into print and *Howlings* was conceived to tip the balance from the purely academic and biographical obsessions of the establishment, and give voice to the radical work we knew was being performed in the living magickal community. *Howlings* was also charged with a specific designed intent, which we

continue to pursue, moving away from the 'dark' occult tome towards an aesthetic of beauty, form, and function, harmoniously conjoined. This informs their entire creation, from design and typography to the materials which we choose to work with. This work supports the fine book arts and traditional skills that are being lost in a world of mass production.

Our mission with Scarlet Imprint is to champion new writers alongside those already established, to encourage dialogue and cross-fertilization. We want to show that there is not one true way, but rather there are a multiplicity of creative approaches, which blur the artificial tribal boundaries that have been staked out between magick, witchcraft and paganism.

As interest in our work grew, it became clear that there are many practitioners and students who cannot afford our hardback or fine editions.

Bibiliothèque Rouge makes our books available to all, unlimited and in a budget format. Our priority is that the ideas and work of our writers takes root in and supports the modern pagan and occult communities. It is also a response to the changing conditions in the world; perhaps our Work with Babalon makes us a little more apocalyptic than others, but our feeling is that we have entered a critical time in our relationship with the world and with Nature. It would not be appropriate to restrict information or cultivate exclusivity, and indeed this has never been our intent with Scarlet. We have now expanded Bibliothèque Rouge to include digital versions of our work, in a further commitment to make the material available and in keeping with the spirit of the information age. We are the only talismanic publisher to do so as far as we are aware, as we believe that the value of the work is not in the creation of artificial scarcity.

*What is the process of transforming simple books into talismanic objects?*

People tend to fixate on the end of the process, the act of consecration, and this is a mistake. The creation of a magickal book begins far earlier. A good analogy is a boxing match, though what happens in the ring is of utmost importance, the outcome of the fight is decided months in advance, in all of the preparation which leads up to the first blow being struck. In this, it is the boxer who trains with intent in every preceding action who will triumph. Magick is about impeccable acts and a magickal book is the result of thousands of processes, each carried out with awareness.

As with stage magic, much of what we do is deliberately concealed. If we were to delineate and deconstruct the book, it would not reveal the mystery, just as vivisection does not truly tell us about the living animal. There are

clear implications in the use of colour, material, binding, and typography. These are the signatures of the indwelling spirit of the book, not simply aesthetic choices.

As with all talismans there is a need for a timing element, something explained clearly in *Picatrix, Key of Solomon,* et al. For a talisman to function, it must be prepared in the right way at the right time. This necessarily differs with every book; as a result, all of our books have a very different feel to them and specific magickal tasks. Here is also the issue of number, another important part of the symbolic calibration and all of our hardback and fine editions are numbered by hand with specific inks. Some also have additional inclusions, which we prefer not to describe.

Smoke is another thing that we can talk about, as suffumigation forms an essential part of the talismanic art. When we worked with the Goetic incense blended for *Howlings,* we encountered more inhuman figures on our way to post the books than actual people! Perfume is critical to evocation.

This talismanic art was once central to magick, but is now neglected, as if circle work is the only valid approach. We know that the living impact of these books will encourage others in their creation of talismans of their own, not simply books. This knowledge has been carried to us through the grimoire tradition, where the procedures and principles are clearly laid out. It is then the individual art of the practitioner, which

must be harmoniously distilled into the object to raise it into independent life.

From our correspondence with our readers, we know that the simple possession of these books can trigger cascades of synchronicities, encounters, and initiation. From a Pomba Gira sashaying past to miraculous escapes from car crashes, from collapse of old certainties to the glimpses of new futures, there is a certain risk in inviting these spirit houses into your life. This has incidentally proved as true of the paperbacks as the fine editions. We take equal care over them all.

Knowledge is not guaranteed with even the most beautiful library of vellum-spined treasures. It requires that it is embodied. The book knowledge must become body knowledge. The simple art of reading is the beginning of a process of transformation, and not the end. Read the words aloud, invoke the spirits from the books and recognise them in the world around you and in yourself. This is after all, a living and unfolding art.

*Witchcraft and magick traditions have their roots in ancient soil, but we are living in the 21st century. While some might think that modernity demands that these things ought to fade away, instead there is a resurgence of interest in the occult. Is the art evolving, are we a part of a story which still has many chapters to write or are we bound only by the past?*

Traditions evolve. There is no seal on the prophetess; the divine revelations are continually given tongue. Repetition of form is meaningless, unless it is filled with living breath; this is magick. Modernity has failed to answer the challenge of spirit and has failed in its stewardship of the natural world. Witchcraft and magick are returning with a vengeance.

Without history, our capacity to know who we are is severely compromised, so we recognise the value of tradition, but not at the expense of ignoring new green shoots from the old tree. Our practice must be relevant and engaged with the world we find ourselves in.

Witchcraft and magick are undergoing a renaissance not witnessed since the Golden Dawn, with a fresh understanding of the role of the grimoires in transmitting knowledge from the ancient world; an infusion of life from the African Diaspora religions; and the boundary transgressing enthusiasm of Western practitioners. There is dramatic and ground-breaking work going on which promises to raise us from a revival to a revolutionary and living current. There is both more to write and to embody.

Humankind is by nature innovative and evolving and it would be a mistake for us to think that tradition itself does not change. As a result of this, we can claim both tradition and continual renewal, the immortal rose flowering out of soil enriched with blood and ground bone.

*Can you speak to our* Almanac *readership about aspects of magickal practice that transcend individual levels of attainment? In this, I mean to elicit your sense of immutable truths that could be useful on the journey for anyone, whether they simply have casual interest or are seasoned practitioners?*

No matter where one is – or thinks one is – on the path, there are certain perspectives, attitudes and practices which are eternally valuable. To retain the mind-set of a student, to be receptive, flexible, honest, and self-examining. Daily practice, self-discipline, and devotion are the key. These deceptively simple acts may elude those who are beguiled by the idea of complexity. Keep a sense of humour, understand the value of friendship and community and empathy and Love. Ensure that there is a physical component to your path, whether yoga, martial arts, rock climbing or running, or gardening. Develop your intent, but not to the detriment of your intuition. Read voraciously and widely. This is your path, not anyone else's. Do not delay, begin this moment. Finally, and vitally, keep going.

*See more of our conversation with Scarlet Imprint when you visit our Almanac extras page at http://The WitchesAlmanac.com/AlmanacExtras/.*

# Notable Quotations
## THE MOON

The moon looks upon many night flowers; the night flowers see but one moon.

*– Jean Ingelow*

I promise to be an excellent husband, but give me a wife who, like the moon, will not appear every day in my sky.

*– Anton Chekhov*

There is nothing you can see that is not a flower; there is nothing you can think that is not the moon.

*– Matsuo Basho*

Moon! Moon! I am prone before you. Pity me, and drench me in loneliness.

*– Amy Lowell*

The moon is a friend for the lonesome to talk to.

*– Carl Sandburg*

Aim for the moon. If you miss, you may hit a star.

*– W. Clement Stone*

Here men from the planet Earth first set foot upon the Moon. July 1969 AD. We came in peace for all mankind.

*– Neil Armstrong*

Tell me what you feel in your room when the full moon is shining in upon you and your lamp is dying out, and I will tell you how old you are, and I shall know if you are happy.

*– Henri Frederic Amiel*

The moon of a bright silver, which dazzles by its shining, illumines a world which surely is no longer ours; for it resembles in nothing what may be seen in other lands.

*– Pierre Loti*

*Quotes compiled by Isabel Kunkle*

# Tom Skelton and a Festival of Fools:

## *A true ghost story or mere tomfoolery?*

EVERY YEAR in late May, hopeful candidates journey to Muncaster Castle in Cumbria, near the River Esk, in England's beautiful Lake District. Muncaster maintains a tradition, honored since medieval times by the Pennington family, in residence for nearly 800 years. Aspirants follow a route traced by visitors since 1325, when the castle was built, to enter a famous contest: the annual competition for the coveted post of court jester. Muncaster is the only castle which still has its own official court jester, also known as the wise fool or clown.

Muncaster Castle is also haunted. Presiding over the community of resident ghosts is that most notorious of all fools, the world famous Tom Skelton.

Visitors to the castle are greeted by Tom's macabre full length portrait, which displays him garbed in his colorful fool's motley, decorative hat and traditional fool's scepter. His face reputedly comes to life, with eyes and lips moving. Tom is portrayed unfurling a long parchment. The document is his will, in which he predicted his own demise by drowning in the River Esk, as well as many other frightening events that  have come to pass. Tom reputedly knew Shakespeare and may have served as the model for King Lear's fool.

It is said that no one could carry off a jest like Tom. In fact, the very word 'tomfoolery' was coined in his honor. Some court jesters were kindly and good humored, like King Henry VIII's fool, the beloved Will Somers. Will went out of his way to delight the poor and cheer the sad. Not so Tom Skelton. Although an extremely clever prankster, Tom was feared. His wit was unexpectedly twisted and often quite cruel. Today, we would call him a practical joker. No one could ever guess Tom or get the better of him. There are hints that he was a gifted psychic.

### The Fool on the Hill

A chestnut tree on a small hill outside the castle came to be called Tom's Tree. The tree is over six-hundred years old and still stands. Tom was reputedly fond of sitting beneath it, watching for passersby. When asked for directions, he often sent them down the wrong path, where they would quickly perish in quicksand at the swampy edge of the Esk. Traditional references to "The Fool and The Tree" or "The Fool on the Hill" were originally subtle warnings which circulated about Tom's treachery.

Sir William Pennington, 16th Century Lord of the Castle and Tom's sovereign, once disliked a suitor preferred by his strong-willed daughter, Lady Heloise. The couple was deeply in love, but the young man was a carpenter from the village, rather than a noble. In 1585, Heloise determined to marry the commoner, despite her father's disapproval. Sir William asked Tom for a trick to end the relationship. Tom secretly followed Lady Heloise, as she left for a rendezvous with her beloved. Discovering where the suitor lived, Tom paid him a visit the next day. He offered to help the young carpenter arrange an elopement and invited him back to the castle for a drink. Tom charmed and entertained his guest with magic tricks and stories, all the while plying him with strong drink. When the gullible teenager passed out at the table, Tom cut his head off, using the unfortunate carpenter's own tools. Always anxious to please his master, the vicious jester then presented the head on a platter. There is no record of the response this elicited. Heloise went mad and was eventually confined to a nunnery.

### Mysterious Footsteps and a Wailing Lady

Visitors to Muncaster tell of hearing footsteps following them, echoing on the stone flooring, accompanied by unexplainable bangs and bumps, although no one is visible. These reputedly indicate the presence of the unfortunate carpenter, still seeking his lost head. Others report witnessing the ghost of a wailing lady, dressed in grey. There are rumors that this is Heloise, returning to mourn her fiancé. The voices of invisible children at play have also been reported.

Historian James Cartland, a friend of the Pennington family, stayed in the castle during the 1980s. He was badly frightened by the presence of ghostly children playing in a room decorated with antique tapestries, relics from Tom's era. Another guest, Lord Carlisle, a 20th Century war hero, was so unnerved by the ghosts of Muncaster that he admitted to curator, Philip Denham-Cookes, that he'd never been more terrified in his life. Lord Carlisle said that he'd had "a terrible night." Patrick Gordon-Duff Pennington, who currently lives at the castle, admits that sometimes it's a happy and normal family home, but at other times, it can be strange and that even the dogs become uneasy.

### A Feast of Fools

The would-be jesters who enter Muncaster Castle's annual competition are jovial and benign, seeking to generate laughter and smiles. Perhaps in an effort to restore the reputation of their profession, they juggle, clown, entertain, tell jokes, and perform magic tricks. Coming from around the world, the prospective fools cheerfully vow to "make fools of wise men and wise men of fools." They ask, "Who among us can determine if there is a difference between the two?"

Muncaster Castle's four-day long annual tournament ends with the famous "Feast of Fools" – a dinner honoring the winner. The official Fool of Muncaster wears the motley (multi-colored costume and belled, tri-cornered hat) for one year. Wi Jem Famous, Maynard Flip Flap, Paul Garbanzo, A. J. James, and Will Tease are but some of the winners. Like his predecessors in earlier times, the current Fool of Muncaster Castle has free reign, allowed to wander the ancient corridors, at liberty to interact with tourists and residents alike. Does Thomas Skelton watch over and critique his or her antics?

– GRANIA LING

# Aleister Crowley

## *Legendary ceremonial magician extraordinaire*

CALLED "the wickedest man in the world" by the press, many who knew Crowley also considered him to be a truly brilliant magician. Born Edward Alexander Crowley on October 12, 1875 at 11:30 PM in England, Crowley's birth chart has both a Sun-Venus conjunction in Libra and a Mercury-Jupiter conjunction in Scorpio in the 4th house of heritage and family. As is usually the case with a strongly aspected 4th house Jupiter, his parents were extremely religious. The Scorpio conjunction also shows curiosity, a fascination with mysteries, and

eloquence. Crowley spent his childhood rebelling against the fundamentalist Christian teachings of the Plymouth Brethren sect, which the family practiced fervently.

As the Libra planets indicate, he was a handsome youth with natural charisma. The Sun and Venus form a T-square aspect with his Mars in Capricorn and Chiron in Aries. This volatile combination of planets hints at his tendency toward violence and lifelong fascination with blood and torture. Before he left home to attend Trinity College, his controversial actions,

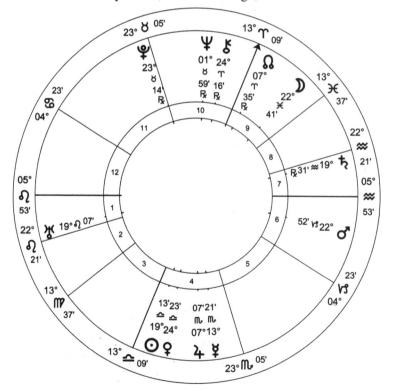

which included animal abuse, led his own mother to brand him as "the beast, the Antichrist."

Pluto in his 11th house shows profound, transformational experiences involving organizations and associates. Crowley left college without a degree, preferring to join The Hermetic Order of the Golden Dawn, a ceremonial magic group. He quickly became adept at occultism. Upon his initiation on November 18, 1898, he took the motto *Perdurabo* which translates "I shall endure." This proved to be most prophetic, for Crowley's writings and his legend are timeless, still revered and referred to in magical circles today. Six planets plus the ascendant in fixed signs in his birth chart indicates great tenacity.

*The Book of Thoth, 777, Equinox of the Gods, Diary of a Drug Fiend,* and *Magick in Theory and Practise* remain among his most popular works. His most important book, Crowley scholars agree, is *The Book of the Law,* reputedly channeled from Aiwass, the spirit messenger of the Egyptian god Horus. The central message of this book is the Law of Thelema: "Do what thou wilt shall be the whole of the law."

The Sacred Abbey of Thelemic Mysteries was the name of his villa in Italy, which was the site of mystical rites. These sometimes degenerated into orgies of such extreme sexual excess and drug abuse that Crowley was deported by Mussolini in 1923. His moon and north node in the 9th house show many changes in residence and refuge in foreign countries. He always seemed more at home and accepted abroad than he did in England.

A prolific esoteric writer and artist, Crowley was also a great talker. In 1917, William Seabrook described meeting Crowley in his book *Witchcraft, its Power in the World Today.*

"Aleister Crowley was a strange, disturbing fellow, with a heavy pontifical manner mixed with a good deal of sly, monkey-like and occasionally malicious humor. He wore an enormous star sapphire on the forefinger of his right hand and sprouted an American Indian warlock which curled slightly and made him resemble (with his round smooth shaven face and big round eyes) a nursery imp masquerading as Mephistopheles."

Crowley's Leo ascendant, with Uranus in Leo in the 1st house, reveals a confident, eccentric, and flamboyant personality with the unusual physical presence, as Seabrook noted.

Of his own poetry Crowley wrote, "England has produced two great poets. Shakespeare was the other one." Mercury is opposed to Neptune in Taurus. This aspect traditionally indicates a prevaricator, one who is not above twisting the truth. Crowley met W. Somerset Maugham in Paris in 1907. He became the protagonist in Maugham's great work *The Magician*. In the introduction to his novel, Maugham wrote of Crowley, "I took an immediate dislike to him, but he interested and amused me. Crowley told fantastic stories of his experiences, but it was hard to tell whether he was being truthful or merely pulling your leg. The odd thing is that he had actually done some of the things he boasted of." Sybil Leek told of meeting Crowley in England. He would visit her family unannounced and always disappear without explanation. Once she saw him outdoors, nearly naked, screaming a hymn to the sunrise.

The genuine psychic phenomena which surrounded Crowley throughout his life is shown by his Pisces Moon in the 9th house, which closely sextiles both Mars in Capricorn and Pluto in Taurus. For a time he called himself Count Vladimir while pursuing occult activities in London. It was then that the reports of demonic manifestations, vampires, supernatural powers, and psychic attacks on his enemies began.

His 7th house of relationships is ruled by Aquarius, with retrograde Saturn there, square Pluto in Taurus and opposing Uranus in Leo. Using a wide orb, these three planets form an angular grand cross with the two Scorpio planets. This describes Crowley's two divorces. Both preceded tragic consequences for his wives. Scandals surrounded his enormous passions. He had numerous mistresses and at least one homosexual relationship, with his magical assistant, poet Victor Neuberg. Saturn-ruled Capricorn is on the cusp of his 6th house of health. The grand cross pattern involving Saturn also describes the forlorn finale to Crowley's life. He battled lifelong ill health, enhanced by decadence and substance abuse, as well as poverty. His writings generated only a modest income.

Although he passed away on December 1, 1947, penniless, insane, ill, and alone, Crowley's work still influences occult practitioners today. Much of the appeal of the path he offers lies in the encouragement he offered about following one's own way. Self observation and experimentation superseding the guidance of a high priest or guru in magical discovery was the essence of his message. Often it proves to be a dangerous one.

– DIKKI-JO MULLEN

# *Aleister Crowley*

*Aleister Crowley was born October 12, 1875
at 11:30 PM in Leamington Spa, Warwickshire, UK*

Birth Data Table
*(Tropical Placidus)*

Sun 19 Libra 13 – 4th house

Moon 22 Pisces 41 – 9th house
(waxing gibbous phase moon)

Mercury 13 Scorpio 21 – 4th house

Venus 24 Libra 23 – 4th house

Mars 22 Capricorn 52 – 6th house

Jupiter 7 Scorpio 07 – 4th house

Saturn 19 Aquarius 31 – 7th house (retrograde)

Uranus 19 Leo 07 – 1st house

Neptune 1 Taurus 59 – 10th house (retrograde)

Pluto 23 Taurus 14 – 11th house (retrograde)

Chiron 24 Aries 16 – 10th house (retrograde)

N. Moon Node 7 Aries 35 – 9th house

Ascendant (rising sign) is 5 Leo 53

# The Naughty Boy – The Saucy Boy

THERE WAS ONCE an old poet, such a good, honest old poet! He was sitting alone in his own little room on a very stormy evening; the wind was roaring without, and the rain poured down in torrents. But the old man sat cosily by his warm stove, the fire was blazing brightly, and some apples were roasting in front of it.

'Those poor people who have no roof to shelter them to-night will, most assuredly, not have a dry thread left on their skin,' said the kind-hearted old man.

'Oh, open the door! open the door! I am so cold, and quite wet through besides – Open the door!' cried a voice from without. The voice was like a child's, and seemed half-choked with sobs. 'Rap, rap, rap!' it went on knocking at the door, whilst the rain still kept streaming down from the clouds, and the wind rattled among the window-panes.

'Poor thing!' said the old poet; and he arose and opened the door. There stood a little boy, almost naked; the water trickled down from his long flaxen hair; he was shivering with cold, and had he been left much longer out in the street, he must certainly have perished in the storm.

'Poor boy!' said the old poet again, taking him by the hand, and leading him into his room. 'Come to me, and we'll soon make thee warm again, and I will give thee some wine, and some roasted apples for thy supper, my pretty child!'

And, of a truth, the boy was exceedingly pretty. His eyes shone as bright as stars, and his hair, although dripping with water, curled in beautiful ringlets. He looked quite like a little cherub, but he was very pale, and trembled in every limb with cold. In his hand he held a pretty little cross-bow, but it seemed entirely spoilt by the rain, and the colours painted on the arrows all ran one into another.

The old poet sat down again beside the stove, and took the little boy in his lap; he wrung the water out of his streaming hair, warmed the child's hands within his own, and gave him mulled wine to drink. The boy soon became himself again, the rosy colour returned to his cheeks, he jumped down from the old man's lap, and danced around him on the floor.

'Thou art a merry fellow!' said the poet. 'Thou must tell me thy name.'

'They call me Cupid,' replied the boy. 'Don't you know me? There lies my bow; ah, you can't think how capitally I can shoot! See, the weather is fine again now; the moon is shining bright.'

'But thy bow is spoilt,' said the old man.

'That would be a sad disaster, indeed,' remarked the boy, as he took the bow in his hand and examined it closely. 'Oh, it is quite dry by this time, and it is not a bit damaged; the string, too, is quite strong enough, I think. However, I may as well try it!' He then drew his bow, placed an arrow before the string, took his aim, and shot direct into the old poet's heart. 'Now you may be sure that my cross-bow is not spoilt!' cried he, as, with a loud laugh, he ran away.

The naughty boy! This was, indeed, ungrateful of him, to shoot to the heart the good old man who had so kindly taken him in, warmed him, and dried his clothes, given him sweet wine, and nice roasted apples for supper!

The poor poet lay groaning on the ground, for the arrow had wounded him sorely. 'Fie, for shame, Cupid!' cried he. 'Thou art a wicked boy! I will tell all good children how thou hast treated me, and bid them take heed and never play with thee, for thou wilt assuredly do them a mischief, as thou hast done to me.'

All the good boys and girls to whom he related this story were on their guard against the wicked boy, Cupid; but, notwithstanding, he made fools of them again and again, he is so terribly cunning! When the students are returning home from lecture, he walks by their side, dressed in a black gown, and with a book under his arm. They take him to be a fellow student, and so they suffer him to walk arm-in-arm with them, just as if he were one of their intimate friends. But whilst they are thus familiar with him, all of a sudden he thrusts his arrows into their bosoms. Even when young girls are going to church, he will follow and watch for his opportunity: he is always waylaying people. In the theatre, he sits in the great chandelier, and kindles such a bright, hot flame, men fancy it a lamp, but they are soon undeceived. He wanders about in the royal gardens and all the public walks, making mischief everywhere; nay, once he even shot thy father and mother to the heart! Only ask them, dear child, and they will certainly tell thee all about it. In fine, this fellow, this Cupid, is a very wicked boy! Do not play with him! He waylays everybody, boys and girls, youths and maidens, men and women, rich and poor, old and young. Only think of this: he once shot an arrow into thy good old grandmother's heart! It happened a long time ago, and she has recovered from the wound, but she will never forget him, depend upon it.

Fie, for shame! wicked Cupid! Is he not a mischievous boy?

Beware of him, beware of him, dear child!

– HANS CHRISTIAN ANDERSEN (1835)

# The Charming Willow

THROUGHOUT THE AGES, the willow has provided a variety of charms and magics. Sacred to Proserpina, Orpheus, Hecate, Circe, Belenus, Artemis and Mercury, willow leaves, bark, and branches are used for healing, inner vision, dream work, and love.

Willow's association with fertility makes it perfect for those in need of a fertility charm. Ancient lore suggests that placing willow branches in an infertile woman's bed will help her to conceive. Likewise, another ancient fertility ritual suggests binding a man to a willow tree with willow thongs and then lashing him around the loins with a willow switch. Willow may also be used in a wonderful spell to attract new love: tradition tells that willow leaves in a hat will not only attract a new

lover, but will also help dispel jealous thoughts felt toward an old lover or jealous thoughts that lover may feel toward you!

## Dreamland and the Underworld

A legend suggests that Orpheus carried willow branches with him while journeying through the Underworld to enhance his gifts of eloquence and communication. So, too, may the poet or musician carry a small bundle of willow twigs to gain inspiration. The use of powdered willow bark as incense may also help spur the creative juices.

Willow is also associated with the dream world. A sprig of willow placed beneath the pillow may help those seeking to increase the potency of their dream magic, as well as those who desire to increase their ability to recall dreams.

You may find that your dreams immediately become more vivid and meaningful.

## Walking the Spirit World

For those who prefer waking walks between the worlds over dream work, incense crafted of sandalwood and willow bark is a very traditional method of facilitating such journeys. In fact, this incense, burned during a waning moon, is greatly helpful in conjuring spirits and communing with them.

For those who walk the spirit world in order to scry, a perfect condenser (an occult infusion of a liquid) can be made by lightly boiling willow, chamomile, and eyebright. This condenser can be applied to your favorite crystal ball or black mirror. It can also be brushed on the eyelids for those who see through visions or swabbed into the outer ears to enhance clairaudience.

## The Willow at Home

A willow planted in your yard protects your home against all sorts of danger and evils. Knocking on the tree, as you leave for your day, helps avert evil that may be heading your way as you travel through your day. And while you're at it, bring some willow branches inside to protect against

any unwarranted sorcery that might be brought into the home, whether carried by yourself or by others.

Of course, having a willow tree right there in your yard allows you to benefit from one of the most traditional wishing trees. From time out of mind, many have sought out a willow with a red strip of fabric in hand, using it to bind their wish to the tree by tying the ribbon to a branch. Once the wish is accomplished, the tree is thanked and the fabric untied. Last but not least, willow wands are considered among the best rods for dowsing for water, earth energies, and buried objects.

– DEVYN STRONG

89

# Chang'e and Jade Rabbit

*Alone together on the moon*

CHANG'E HAD IT ALL: a palace in the heavens, immortal life, and a husband, Houyi the Archer, highly favored by the gods. That is, until Houyi accidentally killed the Jade Emperor's favorite son while hunting in the mountains. Seething with rage, the Emperor cast both Houyi and Chang'e to Earth, condemning them to the mortal realm.

Chang'e was devastated by her quick descent and spent her days looking longingly up to the sky. Every day she grew older and older and it frightened her to no end. Never before had she had reason to fear death: now, it consumed her every thought. Try as she might to hide her unhappiness from her husband, Houyi could not help but feel his wife's anguish. So he made a pilgrimage to the Queen Mother of the West and begged for her help. Touched by his love for Chang'e, the Queen Mother gave Houyi the elixir of immortal life, instructing him to take half for himself and save half for Chang'e.

When Houyi returned, he couldn't wait to give Chang'e the elixir. He had not yet taken his half because he wanted to be with Chang'e when he felt the warmth of immortal

life returning to their limbs. But when he entered their home, he was horrified to see Chang'e being held at knifepoint by some petty thief! Houyi rushed in to save Chang'e and in no time vanquished the thug – but not before being mortally wounded by the thief's blade. With his final breaths, he gave Chang'e the elixir and instructed her to take the whole bottle. When Chang'e swallowed the last drop, she began to float – she had taken twice the necessary dose to induce immortality and was now floating back to her heavenly palace. But alas! The Emperor would not allow her to return and Chang'e became stranded on the moon.

Chang'e began to cry at the thought of an eternity spent alone when she heard a faint tapping. She looked down to see Jade Rabbit hunched over a mortar and pestle, studiously mixing the very elixir that brought her to the moon! Chang'e embraced Jade Rabbit and thanked him for his elixir. Ever since, Chang'e has been helping Jade Rabbit mix his medicines and on still nights, under the full moon, you can hear the tapping of their mortar and pestles.

– TENEBROUS RAE

# The Rollright Stones

*A relic hoar of very ancient time,*
*Of days so long ago that e'en*
*Its very origin is now in mys'try lost,*
*Yet in tradition's oft told tale*
*There's many a worthy truth enshrined*
*Half hid and dullo, like ruby's fire*
*When from the cov'ring clods of earth disclosed.*

*– Excerpt from* Jerusalem *by William Blake*

ON AN ANCIENT site, two miles from Long Compton, England, stands an army of pitted, lichen-covered stones that, on full moons, are said to reassume the form of ancient warriors, who dance to a nearby stream to quench their thirst. Legend has it that these stones are the conjurations of a witch, who blocked an invading king and his army saying, "Seven long strides shalt thou take and if Long Compton thou canst see, King of England thou shalt be."

With the village just over the hill, the king advanced, shouting, "Stick, stock, stone, as King of England I shall be known!" Upon his seventh stride the earth rose up, blocking any view of the town.

"As Long Compton thou canst not see," the witch cursed, "King of England thou shalt not be! Rise up stick and stand still stone, for King of England thou shalt be none. Thou and thy men hoar stones shall be and I myself an elder tree!" With those words, the witch petrified the invaders and then transformed herself into an elder tree – presumably to keep an eye on them.

## The King's Men

Today, one can visit these same stones, the Rollrights. They are composed of a stone circle known as the King's Men, the solitary King Stone, and a portal dolmen called the Whispering Knights. These monuments have stood since the Bronze Age, earning archaeologist William Stukely's description as "corroded like worm-eaten wood, by the harsh jaws of time".

As these stones are located on the oldest known trade route in England, their history has been eventful. Over the last 6,000 years, the stone circle has been raised, rearranged, expanded – and possibly used for cockfights. A 1613 drawing of the King's Men shows an entrance open to the southeast and flanked by two pillar stones that are no longer in place.

It is said that the King's Men cannot be accurately counted, but if they were, the tabulator would be doomed to die within a year and a day. Stories abound of farmers lugging away a stone for a foundation or bridge, only to return it with reports of tragic losses and changes in fortune.

### The King Stone

The King Stone stands on a long mound, 70 yards northeast of the King's Men, just short of the ridge overlooking Long Compton. The King Stone did not always look like a "seal rampant" as it does today. Its current form is the legacy of generations of Welsh drovers, who chipped away protective talismans on their way to market.

While the King's Men have been interpreted as representing a womb, the King Stone is unambiguously male. So much so, in fact, that its reputation has regularly drawn childless women to it during the full moon to rub their breasts against it in exchange for a child – or at least they did before it was fenced in.

In 1895, Dr. A.J. Evans reported locals circle-dancing around it on Mid-Summer's Eve. This is corroborated by William Stukely, who, in 1722, noted a square oblong plot by the stone where, "on a certain day of the year, the young men and maidens customarily meet, and make merry with cakes and ale, the remains of the very ancient festival here celebrated in memory of the interr'd,

for whom the long barrow and temple were made."

Aubrey Burl, a twentieth century archaeologist, noted how tales regarding the Rollright Stones persisted in spite of the church condemning sexual rites and worship of Pagan deities at megalithic rings, chambered tombs, and standing stones since the 5th century CE.

### The Whispering Knights

The Whispering Knights is a portal dolmen with four standing stones and a fifth capstone lying beside them. George Lambrick led an archaeological investigation of the Knights in the 1980s and discovered that they are most likely the oldest of the three groupings. Having been built somewhere between 4000 and 3500 BCE, evidence indicates that it was used as a burial chamber for centuries before it was abandoned, around 1000 BCE.

Although the Rollrights were not a permanent settlement, people may have interred their dead there for several thousand years. In the 17th century, William Stukely recorded additional grave barrows in the vicinity as well, which no longer exist due to agricultural plowing. Just as people today may prefer to bury their dead near places of worship, so these burials lend credence to the theory that the Rollright site was once sacred or a temple. Lambrick found an extensive scatter of relics in the 390 yards between the King's Men and Whispering Knights – many of which did not originate locally. This

*King Stone*

suggests visitors undertook a journey to attend Rollright events.

## The Witch Tree

Given these observations, the witch's role in the above tale deserves further examination. Let's consider the elder tree. Seventeen centuries after the Christian church first forbade the worship of fountains, trees, and stones, the elder tree still demands – and receives – respect. Of all the trees said to house a goddess, few have stronger claims than the elder. She is reputed to be a guardian and a friend to mankind – a reputation that covers much of Eastern, Northern, and Central Europe. Although now seemingly diminished to a dryad or the spirit of a witch, the elder was once revered as a protective mother goddess at Midsummer, when the plant is in full flower.

Aubrey Burl undoubtedly recognized the gossamer threads of ancient veneration when he observed, "frailties of truth in such whimsies, folk-memories fragile as cobwebs, so faint that they are almost undetectable, faded distortion of associations with water, of seasonal assemblies, celebrations. Stories of Pixies who were powerless against iron have been thought to be warped recollections of Bronze Age natives unable to resist the iron swords of Celtic invaders. Others believed fairies to be sanitized tales of witches who had held sabbats in the midnight circle.

How this folklore came about and how comparable unreason still persists despite the increasing awareness of what the stone circle was in prehistory is a pattern repeated at megalithic ring after ring in Western Europe."[*]

Perhaps this is so because the stories speak to a greater truth that lies within us where Mother Nature still chooses who will be her king – or not. Another local Rollright legend suggests that the King and his army sleep in a cavern under the hill, waiting for the day when they will return to rule the land.

## Withstanding Time

Meanwhile, the Rollrights still stand against time. They inspired William Blake to write "Jerusalem" and hosted the Dr. and Romana in the Dr. Who serial arc, *Key to Time*. Locals with "the sight" have seen fairies dancing there; sightings later corroborated by flattened rings of grass. The stones have been neighbors to crop circles and opened their mysterious magnetic energy for dowsers to interpret.

The Rollright Stones have witnessed much. Today, however, Lady Elder must be more diligent than ever; in recent years, the stones have been the target of vandalism and fire damage. Yet they remain open to those that would journey there and can even be rented for seasonal celebrations and Pagan festivals. I recommend Midsummer's Eve, when the elder is in bloom.

– NIALLA NIMACHA

[*]Burl, Aubrey. *Great Stone Circles: Fables, Fictions, Facts*. New Haven: Yale University Press, 1999

# The Art and Magic of Lunar Teas

AS THE MOON exerts enormous influence over water, lunar power can be invoked and harnessed when making tea. Herbalists have long known how powerful the moon's influence can be upon herbal infusions. Brewing beneath the moon imbues the mystery and magic of lunar energy into your brews, potentially enhancing both the properties of the herbs and the intensions fueling your creations.

Lunar teas are potentially wonderful for any need, but are especially beneficial for those issues that are directly affected by the moon, such as ovulation and the female reproductive system. The moon also governs our emotions and subconscious. The potency of infusions brewed for love, meditation, and magical intent is magnified through the use of lunar energy.

### Instructions and Techniques

The basic method for concocting a lunar tea is to gather herbal ingredients, together with a large crystal bowl. If you lack one, use a glass bowl. Have spring water and some cheese cloth at the ready and then head out into the full moon night. You need a location that is unobstructed by trees or buildings, so that your brew can absorb as many hours of moon light as possible.

Place your bowl in your prepared spot. Depending on your intentions, you may now wish to sprinkle rose petals on the ground, sing a song of invitation, or meditate. Once everything has been prepared, pour the spring water into the bowl, filling it half to two thirds full. While pouring, be mindful of the power of water and the pull the moon has over it. Now sprinkle the herbs over of the water's surface. Be mindful of the strength of each herb as well as the chemistry created between your ingredients. Meanwhile, always keep your goals and intent at the forefront of your consciousness.

## Enhancing your Brew

Once all the ingredients are in the bowl, cover it with cheese cloth, so as to obstruct bugs and debris. Allow your brew to steep. If inclined, you can meditate over your brew. Research suggests that this physically alters the molecular structure of water, enhancing its powers of healing. You may wish to surround your bowl with candles, objects such as stones and crystals, or plants that have magical properties, but are not safe to drink. You may also wish to surround the bowl with objects relating or belonging to the person for whom the brew is intended.

At dawn, your lunar infusion will be ready to drink. However, depending upon the intensions for crafting your potion, you may also want to leave the bowl where it stands, so as to absorb the energy of the sun. In that case, drink it upon the next evening's moonrise, possibly with someone special!

Using the described method, here are some recipes for common complaints and desires. Adjust recipes as needed to suit your own specific needs and intensions. Remember: when making lunar teas, allow your creativity to flow!

## Lunar Infertility Brew

3 parts Damiana
3 parts Lemon Balm
1 part Dong Quai
1 part Vitex Agnus-Castus
One half part False Unicorn Root

Lying with your partner beside the tea may enhance its fertility properties. This brew is most potent if consumption is timed to coincide with ovulation.

## Lunar Love Potion

3 parts Damiana
3 parts Rose Petals
1 Vanilla Bean
1 part Lavender Flowers
One half part Patchouli leaves
One half part Valerian roots

Sweeten with honey and serve to your intended, either warm or chilled, as you wish and accompanied by chocolate-dipped strawberries

## Tea to Enhance Dreaming

3 parts Lemon Balm
3 parts Passion Flower
2 parts Gotu Kola
2 parts Gingko Biloba
1 part Valerian
1 part Clary Sage

Drink this before retiring the evening after it's brewed. Place a sprig of mugwort beneath your pillow. Gotu kola assists clarity, while gingko helps you to remember your dreams. Be mindful: dream work can sometimes leave you exhausted!

– Linda Patterson

# The Mirror of Matsuyama

CENTURIES ago on the island of Shikoku lived a man, his wife, and their little daughter. One day the man decided to undertake a pilgrimage to Matsuyama, hoping to secure good fortune for his family. The man promised to be careful and to return soon and to bring presents back from the city. He put on his traveling clothes and set off down the road.

He returned two weeks later bearing gifts. For his little girl, sweets gathered from each stop on his pious journey, and for his wife, a gift of rare splendor: a finely embellished bronze mirror. When he handed the mirror to his wife, she shrieked! She had never seen her own reflection before and was clearly confused, but she came to treasure the mirror as her most prized possession.

Years passed and the family lived on happily together, until one day the wife grew gravely ill. As it became clear that she would not recover she asked her daughter to sit by her bed. She handed the little girl the prized mirror.

"Take this, dear child. Whenever you miss your mother just look here and you will see my spirit." With this final declaration the wife passed into the next life.

The little girl was overwhelmed with sadness, but when she looked into the mirror she found her mother was right! There, staring back, was the face of her mother – not pale and gaunt from sickness but once more young and beautiful. She kept the mirror in the sleeve of her kimono so that she could carry her mother's spirit everywhere.

More time passed and the man remarried – but his new wife was suspicious of the little girl. The girl was secretive, aloof, and never smiled at her new mother. One day she caught the little girl huddled over something, whispering. When she asked what she was doing the little girl slipped something in her sleeve and ran away. The new wife became convinced the little girl was cursing her and begged her husband do something.

So the man found his daughter and demanded the little girl surrender the object. Reluctantly, she handed him the mirror.

Her father was puzzled. "Dear girl, where did you find this?"

"Mother gave it to me on her deathbed. She told me that whenever I missed her I could look into the mirror and see her spirit."

The man understood at once what had happened. The little girl mistook her own reflection for the spirit of her mother. The man and his new wife were touched by the girl's innocence and begged her forgiveness for doubting her. The girl forgave instantly and the new family lived the rest of their lives in serenity.

– TENEBROUS RAE

# Hidden Messages in Your Address

*Open the door to happiness*

FROM BOTH a financial and an emotional standpoint, the purchase or rental of a home is the biggest investment and one of the most important decisions most people will ever make. With the real estate market in a roller coaster cycle of surprises and pitfalls and neighborhoods in flux, selecting the perfect haven is perhaps more of a challenge now than at any other time in history. While on the quest to find the right housing (or perhaps store or office space), the buyer will notice that some prospects will be peaceful and welcoming, while others are interesting, sad, or frightening.

In every area there are some buildings that seem charmed, where the residents prosper, while other places are stagnant and shabby no matter how much effort is exerted in repairing and decorating them. Bankruptcy, illness, even death and injury will plague some households, while rumors of ghosts persist with others. Feng Shui experts advise checking on the past history of places as a first step in analyzing the chi or energy field. This can be most helpful in determining what one is about to step into. However, there is an easy solution. The secret is encoded in the numbers of the address. Numerology is an invaluable and simple tool for understanding the subtle vibrations and potentials surrounding a place.

Consider only the number on the building itself, not the zip code, street, or city. Those numbers relate to the whole region. All numbers reduce to one of the nine single digits. Just add them up until only one number remains. As an example, let's consider a famous address, 1600 Pennsylvania Avenue, The White House. $1 + 6 + 0 + 0 = 7$. So the presidential home is a 7.

Here are some key words for each of the nine basic numbers, one of which will describe every address.

Numerology and astrology have been closely related since earliest times, so the astro-numerology (the zodiac signs and planets which link to the numbers) is included.

### The Number One
An overall warmth prevails and the sun rules. There's a fresh start, dynamic energy. Residents will become more independent, dramatic, warm, and competitive. The horizon seems limitless. Control the ego though.

### The Number Two
The moon is the ruler. Sentiment, appreciation for domesticity, keepsakes, the kitchen, sensitivity, motherhood and babies are a focus. Watch out for moodiness.

### The Number Three
Expansive Jupiter creates an influence for opportunity. Linked to the trinity and triangle, some numerologists consider three to be the perfect number. Growth, education, luck, and a higher standard of living kick you up a notch here. Avoid dangerous gambles with security, though. Live within your means.

### The Number Four
Saturn's rulership here can indicate working at a home business, serious issues to face, and perhaps demanding or depressing surroundings. Prepare 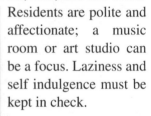 for a reality check, be practical. Patience pays off. Vintage and recycled furnishings can work well. Control negativity and discouragement.

### The Number Five
Mercury-ruled, the five is a busy bee. Conversation, traffic, TV, and a steady flow of visitors can have you saying "never a dull moment." There's laughter and fun, a lively quality, but it's hard to get organized. Avoid getting scattered and giving in to discontent.

### The Number Six
Venus is the patron of the six – it's a love nest. Expect a pretty place, perhaps with flowers, lace, and fine china. Residents are polite and affectionate; a music room or art studio can be a focus. Laziness and self indulgence must be kept in check.

### The Number Seven
Uranus makes the seven a very different kind of space. There can be a history of legends and rumors. A certain loneliness and otherworldliness prevails. Life can take unexpected twists and turns in this exclusive and mystical environment. Gadgets and electronics can be a focus. Overcome loneliness by focusing on fulfilling a personal mission.

### The Number Eight
Neptune and Jupiter combine to make this a really wonderful address for finances and business. Power and accomplishment are likely; the 8 is the cosmic lemiscate. There is recovery from setbacks and an ability to draw upon the reserves of experience. Beware of growing overly materialistic here, however.

### The Number Nine

A cycle is ending; a level is reached. Often the nine is a suitable retirement home. It isn't usually as good for younger families, though. Mars and Pluto combine to create a myriad of possibilities. Residents long to show what they can do. Involvement in politics and community life is likely. Modify, prepare for a new phase, but beware falling into a rut.

IF THERE is a letter on an office suite, home, or apartment, that letter must be factored in using this table of letter-to-number correspondences. Below are the alphabet correspondences used to determine the important numbers in names and words.

| 1 | 2 | 3 | 4 | 5 | 6 | 7 | 8 | 9 |
|---|---|---|---|---|---|---|---|---|
| A | B | C | D | E | F | G | H | I |
| J | K | L | M | N | O | P | Q | R |
| S | T | U | V | W | X | Y | Z | |

### The Pythagorean Table of Alphabet Correspondences

For example, if the address is 301 B, add $3 + 0 + 1 = 4 + 2$ (for the B) = 6. 301 B would be a 6 address.

If you have fallen in love with a building and don't feel drawn to the number's promise, don't despair. Giving the place a name or perhaps adding a letter to the address can modify the original numerology. Use the table above to experiment with different names. What about The Valentine Cottage? Hillcrest? Windy Pines? Let's return to The White House as an example.

### The White House

$1 + 8 + 5 + 5 + 8 + 9 + 2 + 5 + 8 + 6 + 3 + 1 + 5 = 67$. Reducing this further $6 + 7 = 13$ and $1 + 3 = 4$. Reviewing the interpretations of the Four and the Seven, what do you see regarding the nation's first residence?

– Elaine Neumeier

# The Lamb and the Pinecone

ONE TIME, investigating in the backyard of our house in Temuco the tiny objects and minuscule beings of my world, I came upon a hole in one of the boards of the fence. I looked through the hole and saw a landscape like that behind our house, uncared for and wild. I moved back a few steps, because I sensed vaguely that something was about to happen. All of a sudden a hand appeared—a tiny hand of a boy about my own age. By the time I came close again, the hand was gone, and in its place there was a marvelous white sheep.

The sheep's wool was faded. Its wheels had escaped. All of this only made it more authentic. I had never seen such a wonderful sheep. I looked back through the hole but the boy had disappeared. I went into the house and brought out a treasure of my own; a pinecone, opened, full of odor and resin, which I adored. I set it down in the same spot and went off with the sheep.

I never saw either the hand or the boy again. And I have never again seen a sheep like that either. The toy I lost finally in a fire. But even now, in 1954, almost fifty years old, whenever I pass a toy shop, I look furtively into the window, but it's no use. They don't make sheep like that anymore.

– PABLO NERUDA
*excerpt from* Vallejo and Neruda, Selected Poems, *edited by Robert Bly*

# Lycanthropy

## Myths and legends of the werewolf

OF ALL THE LEGENDS and myths surrounding the moon, perhaps none is as frightening as that of the werewolf. Having received numerous Hollywood makeovers, the werewolf – once merely a stock storybook character – has now achieved "classic" monster status and is in the same league as the vampire. The fundamental difference between them, of course, is that werewolves are not the reanimated dead, but are reputedly actual living beings that, when untransformed, look and act just like the rest of us. The technical term for the ability of a human to transform into a wolf is "lycanthropy." How is this achieved?

According to legend, this transformation is typically achieved via magic or through extraordinary events, beyond the individual's control, such as the proverbial "Gypsy curse" or possessing an unfortunate birthday. For instance, children born on December 25 – Christmas Day – have been thought doomed to a life as a shapeshifter, punishment for the sin of being audacious and arrogant enough to share Christ's special day.

### Paw Prints and Lupine Beer

One magical method that reputedly assures transformation is to remove all one's clothing prior to anointing the body with a special magical ointment, made from arcane ingredients, and then donning a wolf-skin belt or tunic. Alternatively, one can drink water collected from a wolf's paw print. A 16th century Swedish belief suggests that lycanthropy is stimulated by reciting a magical formula and then drinking specially-prepared beer. More often than not, however, lycanthropy was considered a curse – an extreme method of divine punishment. The Roman Catholic Church cautioned that the excommunicant would be doomed to wander the earth as a werewolf.

The precise origins of werewolf myths are unknown. The belief that humans can change into animals has existed for centuries. Perhaps the origins of these legends are rooted in animal behavior during the full moon: some dogs demonstrate anxiety, while coyotes and wolves howl at the full moon.

### Not of One Skin

Wolves are not the only creatures into which humans reputedly transform: other were-creatures: include dogs, bears, rabbits, hyenas, cats – even cows! Virtually every culture possesses some sort of were-lore. In Iceland, the locals call such a creature "eigi einhamir" which translates as "not of one skin." These special people – male or female – can, under certain conditions, shrug off their human form and assume another, as easily as changing clothes. An Old English word for such creatures is turn-skin, from which the word turncoat was derived. Today, we refer to untrustworthy people as "wolves in sheep's clothing" – indicating someone who pretends to be what they are not, with ill intent.

But why are there associations between shape-shifting and the full moon? Many agree that on some level, for good or for ill, the full moon does influence human behavior. The general assumption is that, since the full moon exerts a powerful influence on tides, it must also affect the human body. After all, our bodies are 80% water. Romantics swear that we feel more inclined to the pursuit of love during the full moon. By extension, the full moon is also linked to fertility and higher birthrates.

### Lunacy and Lycanthropy

The darker side of this lunar connection is an alleged relationship between full moon nights and increased rates of disasters, crime, and even suicide. Mental illness is also brought kicking and screaming into the equation, hence the terms "lunatic" and "lunacy" – both derived from "Luna" – the Latin word for the moon. There is also, of course, a very real mental illness called "clinical lycanthropy" in which a patient believes that he or she has transformed into a wild animal, typically a wolf, and begins to assume that animal's characteristics.

When I was a child, my maternal grandfather insisted that he was a werewolf. Whether meant as a story to scare the grandchildren (it worked!) or as a way of securing his privacy on full moon nights, I will never be sure. But I do remember that once a month, during the night of the full moon, he would insist that my grandmother lock him in his room and not open the door until daylight.

### A Wild Lunar Landscape

Whether one believes in the supernatural in general, or werewolves in

Werewolf. *Soapstone carving by Clark Ashton Smith, California, 20th century.*

particular, it seems unlikely that we would encounter such a creature in our day and age. Perhaps our shape shifter cousins do exist, but like so many other strange and beautiful creatures have been driven to extinction due to the overpopulation of our planet and the elimination of their natural habitat. Whether one views such habitat as real space, such as the dark storybook forests of old or whether thought of in a metaphorical sense, one thing seems obvious:

We, as human beings, need our wild places and wild things because without them we lack reason to fear. And whether one admits it or not, being afraid reminds us that it is good to be safe. And being safe reminds us of the joys of being alive. From the bright corners of our modern world, we can comfortably look through our curtained windows upon a more mysterious landscape – one which stimulates our intellect as much as it challenges it. The dark spaces between the trees in this metaphorical forest contain not only our fears but our hopes – the shadows become both a reminder of our weakness and an affirmation of our strength. We must remember that things are not always as tidy as they seem to be and that the night, despite its perils, can bring peace and inspiration – especially when illuminated by the full moon.

But meanwhile, just to be sure, I leave you with some antiquated advice – beware a man whose eyebrows meet in the middle, reputedly a sure sign of a werewolf!

– JIMAHL DI FIOSA

# Mysteries and Marvels of the Neem

*A complete pharmacy from the forest*

THE NEEM TREE was once relatively unrecognized and unappreciated, often dismissed as a weed, at least outside of India. Recently, however, neem has emerged as among the most intensely researched and widely appreciated plants.

Neem (*Azadirachta indica*), a member of the mahogany family, thrives in many parts of the world, including the southern United States. An evergreen with slender pinnate leaves, neem is very drought tolerant, growing well even in poor, sandy coastal soil. Neem favors warm weather, thriving best in the subtropics. In regions where temperature dips below 32 degrees Fahrenheit, neem may be cultivated indoors.

Neem grows fast and can quickly reach 65 feet. The tree's wide, bright green canopy enhances well-being. In southern India, neem is known as 'the life-giving tree' because of the shade it brings to yards and homes. In addition to its welcome and soothing shelter, neem is truly magical as it offers so many different gifts, including medicinal, culinary, magical, and spiritual. A staple in Ayurvedic medicine for over two thousand years, every part of the neem – leaves, bark, seeds, roots, and flowers – is considered to have miraculous properties.

### A Passageway to Heaven

Yoga centers and ashrams often carefully nurture a neem tree or two in the belief that, as it grows, so it elevates the spirituality of the property. The *Brihat Samhita* of Varahamihira, a 6th century text, recommends neem highly. Among its verses on plants, this ancient volume suggests that planting a neem near a residence will open a passageway to heaven. Neem leaves are hung in doorways to ward off evil spirits. Smoke

from neem leaves is wafted through nurseries to protect children, while brides infuse their wedding day bathwater with neem.

As the tree is considered sacred, it is traditional for images of various deities to be carved from neem wood pillars. Neem serves as a dwelling-place for the powerful goddess, Kali. Stones are often placed around neem tree trunks to court Kali's favor. Other gods and goddesses are also linked to the neem, among them the fierce serpent mother, Mariamman. She carries a sword shaped like a neem leaf and is  accompanied by a cobra. It is believed that neem trees, planted near a home serve as vehicles for Mariamman's protection against snakes and evil ghosts.

## Culinary and Medicinal Uses

Neem is often used to season food. As a culinary herb, neem is thought to offset the negative effects of the changing seasons and other weather-related maladies, especially extreme heat. Pickled neem leaves are eaten with fish and tomatoes, while young leaves and budding flowers are boiled with tamarind and served as a vegetable. The flowers are fried together with small pieces of eggplant and are featured in a delicious soup recipe. The neem's bitter fresh leaves are chewed on New Year's Day to symbolize the power to make the best of the bad and enjoy the good during the year to come. Some Hindu families exchange neem leaves or flowers of neem for good luck and health.

## Neem Tonics

Neem oil is an effective and nontoxic (to animals, other plants and beneficial insects) insecticide. The warmed oil is also used to treat ear infections, dental, and gum disorders. Neem is added to shampoo to prevent  balding and grey hair. A paste of neem leaves, used as a scalp rub, kills head lice. Neem lotion effectively treats skin disorders. The leaves and tiny twigs are chewed as toothpaste.

## The Tree of Forty

Eating neem fruit expels worms, while eating neem's purple flowers reputedly alleviates stomach disorders. A hot poultice made from neem leaves is used to treat sprains, rheumatism, and swollen glands. In Senegal, neem is used to treat malaria, while in Tanzania, neem is known as 'the tree of forty', meaning that it is thought to cure 40 different medical complaints.

Neem sap is used to prepare food for diabetics and a decoction made from the roots treats fevers. Those suffering from chicken pox and smallpox reputedly find relief by resting on pillows stuffed with neem leaves: like Kali, Sithala, India's goddess of smallpox and other pustulant diseases, also favors the neem.

– ESTHER ELAYNE

# Moon Cycles

*A New Moon rises with the Sun,*
*Her waxing half at midday shows,*
*The Full Moon climbs at sunset hour,*
*And waning half the midnight knows.*

| NEW 2014 | FULL | NEW 2015 | FULL |
|---|---|---|---|
| January 1, 30* | January 15 | January 20 | January 5 |
| February – none | February 14 | February 18 | February 3 |
| March 1, 30* | March 16 | March 20 | March 5 |
| April 29 | April 15 | April 18 | April 4 |
| May 28 | May 14 | May 18 | May 3 |
| June 27 | June 12 | June 16 | June 2 |
| July 26 | July 12 | July 15 | July 1, 31** |
| August 25 | August 10 | August 14 | August 29 |
| September 24 | September 8 | September 13 | September 27 |
| October 23 | October 8 | October 12 | October 27 |
| November 22 | November 6 | November 11 | November 25 |
| December 21 | December 6 | December 11 | December 25 |

\* Black Moon                          \*\* Blue Moon

Life takes on added dimension when you match your activities to the waxing and waning of the Moon. Observe the sequence of her phases to learn the wisdom of constant change within complete certainty.

*Dates are for Eastern Standard and Daylight Time.*

# presage

by Dikki-Jo Mullen

ARIES 2013 — PISCES 2014

ASTROLOGY, the speech of the stars, offers an exalted identification with the wisdom of the universe. Providing guidance for all who trust their course, the pathways in the sky trace the mysteries of life from birth to death. Astrology's insights bring wings to those with open hearts, assuring the ability to soar above disappointments and boredom.

Begin by reading your Sun sign forecast in Presage to discover precisely what this means to you. The entry for your Moon sign will assist you in finding emotional balance, acceptance of family issues, and serenity in processing memories. Explore your ascendant or rising sign forecast to understand your place in the physical world around you. The ascendant tells how others see and react to you.

Throughout the year ahead Saturn, the celestial taskmaster, is in Scorpio. It will be in mutual reception with Pluto, the zodiacal transformer, which is in Capricorn. Mutual receptions occur when planets transit each other's ruling signs simultaneously. Mutual receptions allow the planetary influences to change places and are most auspicious. The mutual reception between these key planets indicates human and animal adaptation to global changes. This leads the way to experiencing good fortune in the face of the adjustments in the ecological and economic climates during the year to come. On November 3, 2013 a rare solar hybrid eclipse occurs. Near that time, just after Samhain, the positive mutual reception between Saturn and Pluto will be especially active. Be alert to the situations described in your own Presage forecasts near that date for important clues about making the most of what the universe provides.

# ASTROLOGICAL KEYS

## Signs of the Zodiac
### Channels of Expression

ARIES: fiery, pioneering, competitive
TAURUS: earthy, stable, practical
GEMINI: dual, lively, versatile
CANCER: protective, traditional
LEO: dramatic, flamboyant, warm
VIRGO: conscientious, analytical
LIBRA: refined, fair, sociable
SCORPIO: intense, secretive, ambitious
SAGITTARIUS: friendly, expansive
CAPRICORN: cautious, materialistic
AQUARIUS: inquisitive, unpredictable
PISCES: responsive, dependent, fanciful

### Elements
FIRE: Aries, Leo, Sagittarius
EARTH: Taurus, Virgo, Capricorn
AIR: Gemini, Libra, Aquarius
WATER: Cancer, Scorpio, Pisces

### Qualities

| CARDINAL | FIXED | MUTABLE |
|---|---|---|
| Aries | Taurus | Gemini |
| Cancer | Leo | Virgo |
| Libra | Scorpio | Sagittarius |
| Capricorn | Aquarius | Pisces |

CARDINAL signs mark the beginning of each new season — active.
FIXED signs represent the season at its height — steadfast.
MUTABLE signs herald a change of season — variable.

## Celestial Bodies
### Generating Energy of the Cosmos

Sun: birth sign, ego, identity
Moon: emotions, memories, personality
Mercury: communication, intellect, skills
Venus: love, pleasures, the fine arts
Mars: energy, challenges, sports
Jupiter: expansion, religion, happiness
Saturn: responsibility, maturity, realities
Uranus: originality, science, progress
Neptune: dreams, illusions, inspiration
Pluto: rebirth, renewal, resources

## Glossary of Aspects

*Conjunction:* two planets within the same sign or less than 10 degrees apart, favorable or unfavorable according to the nature of the planets.

*Sextile:* a pleasant, harmonious aspect occurring when two planets are two signs or 60 degrees apart.

*Square:* a major negative effect resulting when planets are three signs from one another or 90 degrees apart.

*Trine:* planets four signs or 120 degrees apart, forming a positive and favorable influence.

*Quincunx:* a mildly negative aspect produced when planets are five signs or 150 degrees apart.

*Opposition:* a six sign or 180° separation of planets generating positive or negative forces depending on the planets involved.

## The Houses — *Twelve Areas of Life*

1st house: appearance, image, identity
2nd house: money, possessions, tools
3rd house: communications, siblings
4th house: family, domesticity, security
5th house: romance, creativity, children
6th house: daily routine, service, health
7th house: marriage, partnerships, union
8th house: passion, death, rebirth, soul
9th house: travel, philosophy, education
10th house: fame, achievement, mastery
11th house: goals, friends, high hopes
12th house: sacrifice, solitude, privacy

# Eclipses

Eclipses generate changes and surprises. A birthday within three days of an eclipse augurs a time of growth. There will be five eclipses this year. A total eclipse is more influential than a partial.

| | |
|---|---|
| April 25, 2013 | Full Moon Lunar in Scorpio, north node–partial |
| May 9, 2013 | New Moon Solar in Taurus, south node–partial |
| May 25, 2013 | Full Moon Lunar in Sagittarius, north node–partial |
| October 18, 2013 | Full Moon Lunar in Aries, south node–partial |
| November 3, 2013 | New Moon Solar in Scorpio, north node–total |

## Retrograde Planetary Motion

The illusion of apparent backward planetary motion is created by the Earth's speed relative to the other planets. Astrologically, it assures a change of pace.

### Mercury Retrograde Cycle
Impacts technology, travel, and communication. Complete old projects, revise, review, and tread familiar paths. Gemini and Virgo are most affected.

June 27 – July 21, 2013
in Cancer
October 22 – November 10, 2013
in Scorpio
February 7 – 28, 2014
in Aquarius and Pisces

### Venus Retrograde Cycle
Impacts the arts, finances, and love. Taurus and Libra are most affected.
December 22, 2013 – February 1, 2014
in Capricorn

### Mars Retrograde Cycle
Impacts the military, sports, and heavy industry. Aries and Scorpio are most affected.
March 2 – May 20, 2014 in Libra

### Jupiter Retrograde Cycle
Impacts large animals, speculation, education, and religion. Sagittarius and Pisces are most affected.
November 8, 2013 – March 7, 2014
in Cancer

### Saturn Retrograde Cycle
Impacts elderly people, the disadvantaged, employment, and natural resources. Capricorn and Aquarius are most affected.
February 19 – July 8, 2013
in Scorpio
March 2, 2014 – July 20, 2014
in Scorpio

### Uranus Retrograde Cycle
Impacts inventions, science, electronics, revolutionaries, and extreme weather. Aquarius is most affected.
July 18 – December 18, 2013
in Aries

### Neptune Retrograde Cycle
Impacts water, aquatic creatures, chemicals, and psychic phenomena. Pisces is most affected.
June 8 – November 14, 2013
in Pisces

### Pluto Retrograde Cycle
Impacts ecology, espionage, birth and death rates, nuclear power, and mysteries. Scorpio is most affected.
April 13 – September 21, 2013
in Capricorn

# ARIES

The year ahead for those
born under the sign of the Ram
**March 20–April 19**

A fiery natural leader, quick to act and speak, Aries keeps life moving. The Ram seldom wastes time holding a grudge or dwelling on the past. Each new day brings a fresh start, a time to welcome a myriad of novel possibilities.

Spring dawns with the Sun, Venus, Mars, and Uranus dancing together in your birth sign. Your energy level is high; love prospects and great opportunities abound until May Eve. Your 2nd house of finances is accented through May. You'll work hard to enhance income and acquire desired possessions. June 1 – August 8 Mercury makes a passage through your home and family sector. Discussions revolve around home improvements and decisions about residence. Prepare a house blessing at the summer solstice and reinforce it at Lammas to assure peace and plenty for loved ones. Visitors suggest interesting ideas and offer valuable insights during casual conversation, especially just after the New Moon on July 8.

Favorable Mercury and Sun aspects enhance the first three weeks of August. Communication with children as well as hobbies, sports, and creative projects

blossom. August 28 – October 15 finds Mars, your celestial ruler, in your fellow fire sign of Leo in harmony with Uranus. This is a very progressive pattern. Your workload is eased by new technologies and inventions. A competitive spirit encourages you to be progressive and to experiment. Since your 5th house of love is involved, an important relationship intensifies. Light a deep rose-colored candle at the autumnal equinox and dedicate it to a favorite love goddess. The Aries Full Moon on October 18 is an eclipse and engages the Moon's south node. Be aware of your own aptitudes. Do some soul searching to determine how best to be who you are, do what you can, and want what you have. By All Hallows Eve changes in the status quo develop. Flexibility is the key to making the most of new surprises the universe offers.

Early November finds Venus beginning a long passage through your 10th house of career, which will last into late winter. Express creative ideas at work. It's a wonderful time to combine business with pleasure. One who admires you can offer a valuable recommendation leading to a promotion. At Yuletide bless a small potted pine tree and place it in your work space. Doing double duty as a seasonal decoration, it will promote growth and stability to bless your New Year.

January opens with an abundance of cardinal sign energy emphasizing situations which demand immediate attention. Mars in your opposing sign of Libra leads the way, bringing inspiration and suggestions from assertive individuals. This transit lasts through the rest of the winter. The words and actions of others push your buttons. Be sure to get all sides of the story before acting if controversy arises. A legal or ethical dilemma might need attention near Candlemas.

February 7 through March 1 finds retrograde Mercury in your 12th house along with Neptune. Dreams reflect past life recollections and provide insights concerning your path. Invoke an angel or spirit guide for assistance and protection. On March 2 Mars turns retrograde. Be aware of how repeating habits and patterns affect your life's path for good or ill. Examine the past if you would know the future. Winter's final weeks find Venus in your 11th house. Politics, community activities, and new friendships link to long-term goals. Mid to late March is a marvelous cycle for networking.

## HEALTH

With progressive and electrical Uranus midway through a long transit in your birth sign, nervous energy abounds. Take time to release stress. Temperature extremes impact your health. Focus on ways to beat the heat during the summer. After Samhain resurrect a vintage afghan lovingly knitted long ago. Wrap it around you to offset the chills and cold of deep winter. The Full Moon of March 16 brightens your health sector. Chronic health situations can take a turn for the better or promising new treatments can surface near then.

## LOVE

It's truly a summer of love for you. Venus enters your romance sector shortly after the summer solstice. A family member arranges a party or other event which can be a catalyst for a new relationship to blossom. Prepare an intimate Valentine dinner by candlelight on February 14 for one whom you would woo. The Full Moon brightens your 5th house of pleasure that night. Deepest feelings are exchanged and a relationship's potentials are revealed.

## SPIRITUALITY

Neptune, the most mystical and spiritual of planets, remains in your 12th house all year. Personal reverie and deep meditation can be a part of your ongoing spiritual journey. Visit an ashram or retreat center to facilitate a spiritual awakening. The faith of your childhood, a return to your earliest spiritual teachings, can widen perspectives and reinforce your spiritual beliefs while Neptune is retrograde from early June through mid-November.

## FINANCE

The solar eclipse in your 2nd house on May 9 profoundly affects your finances for the remainder of the year. Plan to develop a new, salable job skill. Your income can derive from a different source. Be aware of how changes in the world situation affect your earning potential. It's a cycle during which reading the signs of the times is vital to making the most of resources available. Your values are changing too. A different attitude toward money and which possessions really matter comes into play.

# TAURUS
The year ahead for those
born under the sign of the Bull
**April 20 – May 20**

With unbelievable patience, The Bull waits and persists, usually reaching desired goals through sheer endurance. Determined, careful Taurus appreciates creature comforts and cherishes the finer things in life. This includes music, jewelry, gourmet cuisine, and gardens.

On the vernal equinox Venus, your ruler, changes signs and makes a dynamic square with Pluto, an influence which lasts through the New Moon on April 10. Both business and personal relationships reach a turning point. Hidden factors are revealed to change your opinions and perspectives. Detective and research skills serve you well. From mid-April to mid-May favorable Earth sign transits, including a conjunction from Mercury, promise peace and happiness. Problems and arguments are resolved. Accept invitations to travel near your birthday. The solar eclipse in your own sign on May 9 accents changing priorities. This birthday promises a progressive and exciting year ahead.

Late May through June benevolent influences from Jupiter, Mars, and Venus cluster in your 2nd house of cash flow. Effort is rewarded; finances improve. Make the most of an opportunity to add to your income. The week of June 8 highlights the specifics. On Midsummer's Day light a golden candle and prepare a prosperity talisman. Cinnamon and frankincense sprinkled over a green stone to carry in a medicine bag would be an easy and potent choice. July begins with Saturn changing direction in your 7th house of partnership. Summer's long, bright days find a close partner overcoming an obstacle and preparing to move forward. Your support and encouragement will be appreciated and will inspire a commitment.

July 23 – August 16 Venus brightens your sector of love and leisure. Plan a vacation, perhaps in pursuit of a romantic interlude. At Lammastide offer the fruits of early harvest to honor goddess Habondia and request a boon. By the autumnal equinox an answer arrives. From mid-September through October 7 Venus will aspect Jupiter, Saturn, and Neptune and form a grand trine in water signs. You will delight in the accomplishments of a close friend or partner.

A supportive Mars aspect brings renewed energy from mid-October to December 7. Projects which were once laborious are easier to complete. Make a social occasion of doing chores by asking a friend's assistance. Your creativity is blossoming. If you have a yen to try crafts, painting, or sculpture, this is the time. The Taurus Full Moon on November 17 ushers in a remarkable month. It forms a grand trine in Earth, your element, with planets in Capricorn and Virgo. Trust your hunches, and reach out to those who can help you attain your goals. A friendly rapport with powerful earth elementals such as gnomes and brownies, maybe even The Green Man, lends confidence and a touch of magic to your quest.

Yuletide finds Venus in your 9th house, where it will remain through March 5. Be tolerant of others' spiritual beliefs. It's not the time to be too forceful if debating religion or foreign affairs. Returning to school would be a wonderful idea. It's also a terrific time for overseas journeys. At both the winter solstice and Candlemas decorate the altar with ornaments honoring faraway places and other cultures. A visit from Chiron comes through a dream or moment of reverie in the cold at the dead of night bringing timely advice. Heed the counsel offered. During February Mercury retrogrades in your 10th and 11th houses. There can be some confusion regarding goals and emotions involving your career. Explore options, but wait until early March to initiate change. From March 6 through winter's end Venus transits your midheaven, ushering in a more congenial and uplifting career situation, perhaps with improved working conditions.

## HEALTH

All year the south node conjoins your birth sign, affecting the 1st house. Observe how your own choices are affecting your health. Are you doing all you can to facilitate fitness? Or is your infamous sweet tooth acting up to add to your girth? Self awareness and willpower hold the keys to wellness now. September paves the way to improved health.

## LOVE

Near your birthday a Venus-Sun conjunction brings the promise of romantic bliss. On May Eve try aromatherapy to speed things up. Spray a mist or burn incense using gardenia, ylang ylang, orange, or rose. A Saturn opposition this year hints at an age difference. Don't rule out finding happiness with an attractive someone who is a generation (or more) older or younger. While Venus is retrograde December 22 – February 1, don't change your relationship status. Keep love expressions light and friendly. An old flame can reignite, but a past pattern is likely to repeat.

## SPIRITUALITY

Pluto is beginning the second decanate of a long passage through your 9th house of philosophy and higher thought. Mystery school training, including delving deeply into tarot symbolism, can expand your spiritual horizons. Explore the Cabala. Depth and truth figure in with your spiritual preferences. Draw down the Capricorn Full Moon on June 23 to illuminate your spiritual path.

## FINANCE

From the vernal equinox through June 25 Jupiter, the most benevolent of planets, will move through your financial sector. Devote the springtime to pursuing new avenues of income or making the most of present opportunities. It's truly a "make hay while the sun shines" season and an optimum time to pay off debts. Form new financial strategies.

# GEMINI
The year ahead for those
born under the sign of the Twins
**May 21 – June 20**

Changeable and restless, Gemini is multi-faceted. You assume a variety of different faces. Duality is the theme of your life. Pursuing two or more different jobs or avocations will appeal. Always the zodiac's experimenter and investigator, you enjoy examining ideas and have a flair for communication.

Throughout the spring Jupiter will be completing a conjunction with your Sun. You're experiencing a growth spurt. An underlying sense of being jolted from your comfort zone prevails. Rise to the occasion. Your horizons are widening. You might sense a completion or release linked to a project or relationship you've outgrown. It's time to move forward. The vernal equinox brings a dreamy but scattered mood. Mercury, your ruler, will square your Sun and conjoin Neptune March 20 – April 13. Organize your surroundings with a feng shui session. Donate items you haven't been using to a worthy cause and you'll experience good karma in return.

From late April through mid-May a strong 12th house influence accents charitable endeavors. At Beltane prepare a blessing to benefit animals or people in need. On May 10 Venus enters your birth sign, followed by Mercury. Social prospects brighten while the spring days grow longer and sunnier. Pursue travel, art appreciation, and learning experiences. The Gemini New Moon on June 8 grants a cherished wish and emphasizes friendship.

From the summer solstice through late August your financial sector is accented; a retrograde Mercury cycle and Mars transit are involved. Give thanks for your possessions at Lammastide. Your financial history offers clues to improving your security now. Keep receipts for major purchases in case a refund or exchange is needed. A contact connected to an old job or a salable skill acquired in years past can become a financial blessing.

September 1 – 9 brings a focus on real estate as well as heritage and family life. Communicate with relatives concerning home improvements. The New Moon esbat on September 5 would be a wonderful time to bless your dwelling, perhaps with a sage smudge. By the autumnal equinox leisure time activities and romantic trysts are a focus, as your 5th house of pleasure is highlighted by Mercury and the Sun. Relationships with young people are uplifting. Finalize plans for Samhain festivities by October 22. A fairy tale character provides inspiration for your Halloween costume.

The solar eclipse on November 3 emphasizes the role of animal companions. A beloved familiar appreciates extra time and attention. November through early December offers insight regarding the best choices for diet and exercise regimes. The Gemini Full

Moon on December 17 accents leadership. You will be aware that others look up to you. Yuletide ushers in an enthusiastic mood involving air sign aspects, which prevails through winter's end. Your vitality improves; winter sports facilitate happy social situations. Walk through a frosty wonderland of pristine snow with one you care deeply for.

January finds a stellium of Capricorn planets, including Mercury, Pluto, and Venus, in your 8th house. Mysteries and all kinds of research captivate you. This might involve communication with a spirit guide or friendly ghost by Candlemas. February finds Mercury turning retrograde in your 9th and 10th houses. Reflect carefully if you're considering a career change. Memories of grandparents or relationships with grandchildren are heartwarming in late February, and any volatile situations with in-laws should settle down. March finds Jupiter completing its retrograde in your 2nd house of finances. An old obligation is completed or a purchase is finalized. Winter's end brings contentment and a positive resolution regarding monetary situations.

## HEALTH

Saturn is in your 6th house of health all year. Patience and an awareness of the impact of past habits pave the way to attaining health-related goals. Examine hereditary and environmental factors for insight. Two favorable north node eclipses on April 25 and November 3 promise improvement in health. Innovative or alternative treatment programs can play a role in this.

## LOVE

Spring's first Full Moon, on March 27, falls in your 5th house of love. It's easy to reveal your deepest feelings; you'll wear your heart on your sleeve. Mars, planet of passion and desire, enters your love sector on December 8 and remains there through the winter. Prepare for a time of excitement and intensity in love. Love philters and charms blessed at the winter solstice and Candlemas can be helpful.

## SPIRITUALITY

Venus has a link to your 12th house, which rules the deepest subconscious mind and the sixth sense. A love connection can make you receptive to spiritual fulfillment; so can spiritual music and art. During May, a Venus transit stimulates these deep, heartfelt feelings of love which promise spiritual transcendence. Try Edgar Cayce's recommended spiritual hues of blue-purples and rose for décor or candle colors to assist in awakening spirituality.

## FINANCE

On June 26 lucky Jupiter enters your financial sector where it will remain through the rest of the year. Additionally, Jupiter will form a grand trine with Saturn and Neptune in water signs. This is marvelous for following your intuition regarding money. Lady Luck promises a turn for the better. The Jupiter-Saturn trine has often been called "the millionaire's aspect." Even if that isn't fulfilled literally, you should experience contentment regarding finances. Your most important material needs and desires will be met.

# CANCER
The year ahead for those
born under the sign of the Crab
**June 21 – July 22**

The receptive and sensitive Crab does best when sidestepping all that is depressing or negative. When in positive surroundings, conscientious Cancer becomes a dedicated and hard worker. Your unusually retentive memory makes you something of a human encyclopedia.

The arrival of spring generates a competitive spirit. Mars is at your midheaven, and the pace quickens March 20 – April 20. Career aspirations are involved. Prepare to embrace opportunities. Timely action can change your destiny. Observe new developments in your field; be inventive. From late April through May 31 a parade of transits in your 11th house will sextile your Sun. A whole network of new acquaintances reaches out to you. An invitation is extended to participate in an organization which is dedicated to a cause you believe in. Think this through before acting. Goals are being selected which could have long-range impact on your future.

June marks a happy cycle. Venus enters your birth sign where it will create a splendid and sociable grand trine in water signs, with Saturn in Scorpio and Neptune in Pisces. Creative gifts are in top form. Plan a party, focus on an intimate relationship, try your hand at watercolor painting, or purchase tickets for the best seats at the opera. On Midsummer's Eve bedeck the altar with crystals, ribbons, and fragrant flowers. Wear jewels.

The New Moon in Cancer on July 8 opposes Pluto. Your birthday month brings a renewed sensitivity to the ecological, economic, and political issues which impact the quality of life for the masses. A perspective on how you affect associates, what you can and can't do with and for them, is a focus. Time spent in nature, especially near the waterfront, facilitates healing and balance. Mercury transits your birth sign from early June through early August. This is an optimum time for travel, decision making, and gathering information. Be a good listener. Invaluable information and advice are presented in casual conversation.

August finds Mars and Jupiter conjunct your Sun. It's imperative to direct your attention toward constructive goals. This is a very powerful planetary combination. Much can be accomplished if righteous anger is applied to make constructive changes. Exercise good judgment regarding risk taking. Prepare for adventures as summer fades into early autumn. September finds a lovely Venus and Mercury influence brightening home and family life. Home improvement projects are a success. Entertain friends and relatives.

The October 18 eclipse in Aries ushers in progressive conditions regarding your career. Changes can be sudden and unexpected. Look toward the future, not back at the past, then all will be well. Many water sign placements at Samhain favor honoring rain and the waves in ritual celebrations. Place a small tabletop fountain on the altar. Select a sailor, pirate, mermaid, or King Neptune Halloween costume.

From November 1 to December 4 Mercury is positive. It's an ideal time to travel for pleasure, whether alone or with a loved one. Visit a bookstore or library. The Yuletide season brings a grand cross in the cardinal signs. A sense of urgency prevails. Release stress. A yoga session would help keep you from feeling overwhelmed. Wear a peace symbol or inscribe a parchment with harmonious runes at the winter solstice to cope with an exciting yet unsettled holiday.

The first Full Moon of 2014 falls near midnight, late on January 15, in Cancer and coincides with a Venus-Jupiter opposition. An intimate relationship is a catalyst for wish fulfilment. Others introduce you to philosophical truths and cultural experiences. A sense of destiny prevails following the lunation. In February Mercury hovers near a conjunction with Neptune in your 9th house. This favors spiritual studies. Read poetry at Candlemas. On March 2 Mars turns retrograde in your 4th house of domesticity, where it remains through winter's end. Take normal precautions to assure household safety. A family situation is resolved satisfactorily.

## HEALTH
Jupiter, ruler of your health house, enters your birth sign on June 26 and remains there through the end of the year. Overall, this is a favorable indicator for health. However, Jupiter does rule expansion and can indicate overindulgence. Limit portion sizes to avoid unwanted weight gain. As a water sign, you'll always benefit from drinking plenty of water or having a relaxing soak in an herbal bath.

## LOVE
On April 24 and November 3 favorable north node eclipses highlight your 5th house of love. This promises twists and turns for the better in relationships. The year brings sparkles and surprises regarding love. Sudden meetings and partings play a part in the romantic drama.

## SPIRITUALITY
Neptune, Jupiter, and Saturn aspects link with the Full Moon on September 19. This magical lunation facilitates spiritual consciousness. Dream recollections, water elementals, and past life memories create a tapestry of insight. Draw down the Harvest Moon. Follow up with a deep meditation at the autumnal equinox to attune to the Moon's wise counsel.

## FINANCE
Your 8th house of financial strategies is ruled by impulsive Uranus, which makes some rough aspects in your chart this year. Excessive generosity can create a financial pitfall now. Shop for the best values in insurance and carefully check tax records. June and September bring the year's best financial prospects.

# LEO
The year ahead for those
born under the sign of the Lion
**July 23–August 22**

A natural leader, with inherent determination and independence, the dignified Lion is charismatic. With the Sun as your celestial ruler, you are good natured with a sunny disposition. Brightness, warmth, and generosity characterize you.

From the vernal equinox through April there is a focus on distant horizons. Several 9th house placements will trine your Sun, making you anxious to explore and wander. Foreign travel and study programs will beckon. By Beltane, competitive and dynamic Mars will ignite your career sector, a trend which lasts until May 31. Your enthusiasm and motivation propel you forward, but keep a sense of humor and perspective, especially if a situation angers or frustrates you. All eyes are on you. You're the center of attention now.

On June 1 Mercury enters your 12th house where it remains until August 8. Your insight is keen; memories are vivid and poignant, especially near the summer solstice. Plan a traditional Independence Day celebration reminiscent of childhood picnics and fireworks. Periodically throughout July you will savor quiet moments, cherishing chances to release stress. Intuitively you realize that a tranquil mind knows the right answers. June 28 – July 22 finds Venus in your sign. A relationship takes a turn for the better. You'll revel in fashion, art, and music. By Lammastide a Venus-Neptune opposition aspects your 2nd and 8th houses. This relates to income, investments, taxes, and insurance. Clarify financial situations; be wary of advice if something doesn't ring true. Prepare a prosperity candle at the sabbat. After the New Moon in Leo on August 6, Mercury comes to the rescue. Racing through your sign, Mercury waves triumphantly at Uranus which is in your sister fire sign of Aries. This is a free-spirited influence, bringing quick, bright solutions to problems and opening the way for travel and adventure throughout the rest of August.

August 28 through October 15 Mars will conjoin your Sun. This is an intense pattern. Your workload is heavy, but much can be accomplished. Pace yourself and get priorities in order as the autumnal equinox nears. A strong Mars-Saturn square points to some extra responsibilities involving a family member or home maintenance.

On October 8 Venus enters your love and pleasure sector and activates a very favorable grand trine in the fire signs. This bright and creative cycle lasts through November 5. Samhain promises to be especially joyful. Place a crystal on the sabbat altar to honor true love. The solar eclipse on November 3 conjoins Saturn and Mercury in your 4th house of home and heritage. A new perspective concerning family life will emerge during the weeks before

Thanksgiving. A more suitable residence might be needed or your present abode could need redecorating. December finds Mercury joining the Sun in Sagittarius, initiating an upbeat trend which lasts through the winter solstice. Loved ones are easier to communicate with, and decisions about a winter vacation or holiday projects generate joyful anticipation.

Late December through February 1 Pluto and retrograde Venus affect your health sector. Nurture your body with wholesome foods and moderate exercise. Be aware of how emotions or overindulgence can affect well-being. Let the head rule the heart regarding decisions related to animal companions. Postpone adopting a new pet. Healing rituals of all kinds are apropos for Candlemas.

The Leo Full Moon on February 14 accents teamwork and sharing. Your 7th house of partnership enjoys positive influences from transits in Aquarius, your opposing sign, from early February through mid-March. Revel in the success someone close to you enjoys. A legal matter can be resolved in your favor as winter draws to a close.

## HEALTH

Pluto remains in Capricorn, your health sector, all year. This is excellent for rejuvenation and bringing hidden conditions to light. A time of healing commences at the Capricorn Full Moon on June 23. Heed the symbols in your dreams; they describe what your body needs. Saturn makes a square to your Sun this year from your 4th house, accenting the impact that heredity and living arrangements have on your well-being.

## LOVE

From March through the summer solstice, Jupiter, ruler of your 5th house of love, will transit Gemini. You can feel scattered, uncertain, and divided regarding matters of the heart. By your birthday, Venus comes to the rescue. A healthy and loving relationship begins to deepen as summer progresses. On Valentine's Day, February 14, there's a Full Moon in your birth sign. Share a drawing down ritual with a dear one to bless a cherished union.

## SPIRITUALITY

Your awareness of other dimensions is expanding. Neptune is moving deeper into Pisces, ruler of your 8th house of mystery, all year. Since this is a water sign influence, walks along the shore or meditation on a rainy day can stimulate spiritual awakening. Dance would provide a catalyst for spiritual growth. Try Sufi, Native American, or folk dance. Explore the history and significance of the music and dance steps.

## FINANCE

May brings an eclipse in your career sector. Prepare for changes regarding your profession. Stay on top of the newest trends. Adapt and be flexible. Mercury, the planet of knowledge, rules your 2nd house of cash flow. Discussing and reading about finances will help. Plenty of information is your key to prosperity.

# VIRGO
The year ahead for those
born under the sign of the Virgin
**August 23 – September 22**

Thoughtful, industrious, and serious, Virgo is the zodiac's beloved fussbudget. Idealistic yet practical, your ruling planet is clever, agile Mercury. You strive always to perfect your knowledge and sharpen your skills.

From early spring through April 14 Mercury opposes your Sun from the house of partnerships. Those closest to you express conflicting viewpoints. Discussion and compromise can help to smooth over differences. The last half of April through May Day emphasizes the spirit realm. Several transits, including Mars, highlight mystery and rebirth. Heed subtle omens and synchronicities, especially from Walpurgis through Beltane. Messages arrive from other dimensions, delivered by spirit guardians. On May 2 a potent planetary emphasis on Taurus, your sister earth sign, commences. Through the end of May, favorable aspects for travel and study will carry you forward. During June, Mars will square your Sun while crossing your midheaven, entering the sector of fame and fortune. A competitive mood prevails. Invest extra effort in career goals, and progress will be enjoyed near the summer solstice.

Mercury is retrograde from late June through July 21 and affects your 11th house. This impacts your circle of friends and long-range goals. The New Moon on July 8 brings the specific impact into focus. Reflect and regroup, but delay steering away from established associates or committing to a new direction until Lammastide. During the first half of August, Venus passes through Virgo and conjoins your Sun. This is excellent for social life. Plan a vacation, try a craft project, or enjoy cultural events. The Full Moon on August 20 in your 6th house accents health, your favorite subject. Experiment with wholesome recipes and explore alternative health options during late August.

September 1 – 9 finds Mercury in your sign, making favorable aspects to both Saturn and Jupiter. Employment options are promising; travel is enjoyable and productive. The New Moon in Virgo on September 5 is excellent for finalizing plans and making decisions. As the autumnal equinox nears, your 3rd house is highlighted, a trend which is supported by several transits through December 4. Anticipate some intriguing conversations and messages. Several short journeys are likely. It's a great time to catch up on current events; much is taking place in the world around you. Mercury will be retrograde at All Hallows. Resurrect a vintage costume and celebrate in keeping with established traditions.

The weeks leading up to the winter solstice bring family matters and heritage to your attention. Home improvements, genealogy, or real estate transactions can be involved. At Yuletide prepare a house blessing. From December 25 to January 9 Mercury, Pluto, and the Sun gather in your 5th house. Practical expression of creative ideas, perhaps involving a hobby you enjoy, make this a cycle of contentment. You can analyze and understand a love situation, finding a comfortable balance between the dictates of the heart and head. Remember, in a conflict between the head and the heart, always follow the heart.

Deep winter finds Mars creating a stir in your 2nd house of finances. Expect extra work. Effort will be invested in managing money and acquiring desired purchases. Be constructive; direct your attention toward improving the financial status quo. At Candlemas Venus completes its retrograde cycle. Any uncertainty related to a love relationship should dissolve by Valentine's Day. A sense of teamwork builds during late February and March. On March 16 the Full Moon in Virgo sextiles Saturn. This is excellent for performing esbat rituals blessing time, history, and intergenerational situations regarding elders and the very young.

## HEALTH

Uranus, ruler of your health sector, makes a strong aspect to Pluto all year. This cautions against hasty decisions or aggressive treatments regarding healthcare. Patience and study are essential in order to reach wellness goals. Mars races through Virgo October 16 – December 7. Mars, like fire, can do much good when used properly and great damage when uncontrolled. This is terrific for exercise programs. Motivation and enthusiasm grow. But avoid confrontations or extreme sports during this time.

## LOVE

Venus, the celestial love planet, will join Pluto in Capricorn in your 5th house of romance from early November through early March. This promises a nurturing and meaningful relationship. Share time outdoors with the one you covet. Carry crystals and gems to bless and secure a desired love tryst.

## SPIRITUALITY

Mystical, ethereal Neptune perches in your 7th house of partnerships and forms a grand trine in water signs with Jupiter and Saturn from June 26 through the winter. Attuning to the emotional needs of others accelerates your own spirituality. Sea shells, images of dolphins, mermaids, and angels on your altar provide the perfect spiritual focus. Add a vial of holy water.

## FINANCE

Be wary of gambles, innovative schemes, or risky financial prospects suggested by others. A quincunx aspect involving your sector of insurance, investments, taxes, and inheritance is active. This warns of a potential loss. The lunar eclipse of October 18 reveals the specifics. Trust your own instincts. Winter ends with Jupiter fortunately aspected, indicating that financial needs will be met if you budget and live within your means.

# LIBRA
The year ahead for those
born under the sign of the Scales
**September 23 – October 23**

Pleasant, affable, and even-tempered, Venus-ruled Libra is highly sensitive to the feelings and wishes of others. The Scales, your symbol, hints at an affinity for symmetry and balance. Creative work, public relations, or the legal profession intrigue you.

You will greet the springtime with a volatile and intense relationship situation in progress. March 27, the night of the Full Moon in Libra, offers insights about this. Mars conjoins Uranus in your 7th house of partnership from March 20 to April 20. Meditate on whether to hold on or to just let go and move forward.

On May Eve prepare a green candle for prosperity. Decorate the altar with fresh basil and parsley sprigs to attract abundance. The eclipses on April 27 and May 9 impact your 2nd and 8th houses, affecting finances. Changes are impending regarding money matters. From mid-May through June 25 Gemini transits, led by benevolent Jupiter, will aspect you favorably. The 9th house is highlighted, showing opportunities for travel, perhaps to visit a sacred or historic site. This is a wonderful time to write prose or poetry for publication. Begin a journal.

It might become the outline for a great novel.

From early July through August 22 Venus, followed by the Sun, will brighten your 11th house. New goals arouse enthusiasm. Friends genuinely care for you. You're invited to parties and events. Become more active in an organization or pursue community service. At Lammas do a tarot reading to determine how to overcome uncertainty. You don't want to give in to decision by indecision. From late August through September 29, Venus and Mercury play tag in your birth sign. At the same time both planets will conjoin your Sun. This is a great time to plan a journey, either for business or pleasure. Career prospects are brighter. Heed suggestions offered by others near the autumnal equinox. Communication with loved ones is pleasant and easy near your birthday.

Late October through November 11 Mercury is retrograde in your money sector. Keep receipts and accurate financial records in case you must document transactions or return a costly purchase. Be aware of your financial history. Repeat only those patterns which have proven beneficial. Enjoy upbeat aspects in your 3rd house involving Mercury and the Sun during the first three weeks of December. Plan holiday visits and events. Seasonal correspondence evokes goodwill and happy memories.

From mid-December through the end of winter Mars moves through your own birth sign, adding fire and zest to your life. Enthusiasm and motivation will peak. Much can be accomplished, but keep anger and impatience in check. The strong Mars trend is favorable for beginning a fitness program or perfecting your skills in a sport. Maintain a healthy perspective on competition. Venus, your ruler, turns retrograde at the winter solstice. The sector of residence and family is impacted. Your home might need some redecorating or repairs. Tolerance and humor help in coping with a relative or visitor who is a bit difficult. Seek last-minute holiday bargains.

January finds Mercury racing through your 4th and 5th houses. Get loved ones talking; be a good listener. A change of scene is inspirational. By Candlemas Venus is direct and a grand cross in the cardinal signs, aspecting your Sun, is activated. A dynamic energy prevails. There's a sense of urgency, and many projects need attention at once. Get organized and prioritize.

Early February finds a Mercury-Neptune conjunction affecting the animals near you. Heed a hunch about the well-being of a cherished pet. Also, a new animal may find its way to your door. The last part of February emphasizes a need for clarity. Make time to release stress and clear away clutter. March brings Aquarius transits which trine your Sun, stimulating your sensitivity to color and sound. Try a chakra balancing session, including visualization of the appropriate colors while humming the corresponding musical notes to honor the last weeks of winter.

## HEALTH

Ethereal Neptune remains in your health sector all year. The magic of extra sleep facilitates healing. From June 26 through the year's end, Neptune forms favorable aspects for health treatments involving water. Drink plenty of fluids to detoxify the body. Try foot baths or steep healing herbs in your bath water. A dream reassures you about a health concern near the time of the Harvest Moon on September 19.

## LOVE

Cupid brings your brightest love cycles when Venus dances through the air signs May 10 – June 2, mid-August through mid-September, and March 6 – 19. Watch for a love omen brought by the breezes, perhaps a fragrance, a feather, the laughter of a faerie, or a colored leaf, to answer your questions about a love situation.

## SPIRITUALITY

Spring brings a transit from Jupiter highlighting your 9th house of higher thought. This favorably impacts spiritual awakening. Seek books focused on spirituality. Invoke the guidance of the deities which correlate with Jupiter, perhaps Zeus and Thor, to expand your consciousness. A thunderstorm, along with messages illustrated in cloud formations, reveals a spiritual truth.

## FINANCE

Saturn wades slowly through your 2nd house of finances all year. Patience helps in attaining financial goals. Enjoy what you have. Recycle. Budget carefully, and late winter will open brighter financial horizons. Smudge with sage and pine to stimulate prosperity.

# SCORPIO
The year ahead for those
born under the sign of the Scorpion
**October 24 – November 21**

Shrewd, intense Scorpio relishes life's material and sensual pleasures. Calculating and highly enterprising with a flair for secrecy, you are a gifted detective. Any kind of analysis or investigation, including ghost tracking, is your forte. Your innate skepticism helps you to ferret out the truth.

At the vernal equinox a gentle, sweetly romantic mood prevails. Mercury and Neptune kiss in your love sector through All Fool's Day. A wonderful mental rapport is established with one whom you would woo. The first half of April is a sentimental journey, deepening a close relationship. On April 13 Pluto, your ruler, turns retrograde in your 3rd house, a trend which continues until September 21. This is a wonderful influence for reviewing academic materials in order to complete a course of study or refresh skills. Explore past life situations to develop coping skills involving complex individuals, especially neighbors or siblings.

There is a partial eclipse on April 25 at the Full Moon in Scorpio. Prepare for the unexpected; a change in residence or career focus is likely. Old doors are closing so new ones can open. A strong Mars opposition enters your 7th house with the eclipse and remains until May 31. May Eve is a great time to bless a commitment, as Venus will hover near both Mars and the Sun. Listen to suggestions. Others are competitive and a bit argumentative; focus on tolerance and cooperation. A partner has definite plans and ideas involving you. Consider all sides of situations. Compromise is the key.

On June 1 Mercury enters Cancer, your sister water sign, to begin a long and favorable passage through your 9th house, setting the pace until August 8. Your intellectual gifts are in top form. It's an optimum time to pursue independent study or to enroll in educational programs. Relationships with in-laws or between grandparents and grandchildren will improve. Prepare healing rituals at both the summer solstice and Lammas. Old wounds are soothed.

Leo transits are crossing your midheaven during the last three weeks of August. The light of fame and fortune beams down upon you. Opportunities arise for taking on new challenges. Your highest potentials are unleashed. September is all about love, as gracious Venus enters your sign and remains until October 7. Social prospects are promising; network with new friends. Bless a love token on the altar at the autumnal equinox and honor the fruits and vegetables of early autumn. Prepare apple pie or cornbread.

Throughout October and November there is a powerful influence in the water signs involving Mercury, Jupiter, Saturn, and Neptune aspects to your Sun. Your imagination is at a peak and creativity carries you forward.

Travel, especially by ship or along the waterfront, is fortunate. Nostalgia prevails while Mercury is retrograde October 22 – November 11. Include beautiful sea shells and salt water in a Samhain ritual.

The total solar eclipse in Scorpio on November 3 marks a time of new beginnings. Release the old near your birthday and embrace all that is fresh and unexpected by the end of November. Your 2nd house of money is emphasized December 1 through the winter solstice. Consider new directions concerning salable job skills and budgeting. Financial brainstorming sessions offer valuable perspectives about security issues.

Winter begins quietly. Mars, which co-rules your birth sign, is in the 12th house where it will remain through March. Venus is in a retrograde cycle in your 3rd house December 22 – February 1. You will relish peace and privacy. During meditation you may be inspired to pursue charitable work or a volunteer opportunity. Satisfaction comes from helping those in need. The New Moon on January 30 activates your 4th house of home and family life. This trend remains active until March 1. Seek ways to make your abode more comfortable. Bless your home at Candlemas. How about adding a bagua mirror or anti-evil-eye bead to the household's foyer? The first week of March finds Venus joining Mercury in your home and family sector. Love, harmony, and improved communication prevail at home. Your residence becomes a place of refuge, truly your castle, as winter ends.

## HEALTH

Uranus transits your health sector all year. Control stress. Be patient and pace yourself while working toward fitness goals. The lunar eclipse on October 18 impacts your 6th house of health. There can be breakthroughs and turning points regarding health near then. Heed subtle signals sent by your body and all will be well.

## LOVE

Dreams and hunches reveal the heart's twists and turns this year. Visionary Neptune is affecting your love sector. An idealistic and romantic mood prevails. Forgive and forget a loved one's frailties, and intimate relationships will go well. Late spring and early autumn promise romantic bliss.

## SPIRITUALITY

Explore the spiritual traditions of Walpurgis Night and the witcheries of Germany's Hartz mountains, especially The Brocken. The lunar eclipse in Scorpio on April 25 links to the time-honored magical traditions of this area. If possible, travel to Germany or view a film or photos of these ancient, sacred places to facilitate spirituality.

## FINANCE

Jupiter, ruler of your financial sector, begins a favorable transit on June 26 which lasts through the winter. Your monetary prospects should improve dramatically. Jupiter trines Saturn in your birth sign in mid-July and again in mid-December. This pattern has been dubbed "the millionaire's aspect." Make the most of opportunities for gain then.

# SAGITTARIUS
The year ahead for those
born under the sign of the Archer
**November 22 – December 21**

Self-reliant Sagittarius is forever dedicated to growth and expansion. Ruled by jovial Jupiter, your nature is cheery and generous. Like the Archer aiming at lofty, distant targets, you are competitive and idealistic.

At the vernal equinox, Jupiter highlights your relationships. A partner is in a growth mode and would deeply appreciate supportive words of encouragement. Revel in the accomplishments of someone very close to you. This trend is fortunate for resolving legal issues amicably as well. March 20 – April 20 finds Mars in Aries, making a wonderful fire sign trine to your Sun. Your love and pleasure sector is impacted. Enjoy sports; experiment with creative outlets. Your vitality peaks. You'll be motivated and enthused.

Celebrate May Day by sipping a philter of fresh herbs; try peppermint and lemon balm. During Beltane rites an emphasis on healing and problem solving emerges. You adore animal companions. A relationship with a precious pet deepens. You discover that this connection facilitates healing of your body and spirit. On May 25 the lunar eclipse in your birth sign ushers in exciting new developments in your

life. Under the shimmering moonlight, gaze into a crystal for a vision of who you really are and what your life's purpose is.

June begins with a Mars opposition to your Sun, which sets the pace until July 14. Associates present cherished plans and suggestions. People are assertive. Cooperation is essential to progress now. Devote the summer solstice to a blessing for peace. Let humor overcome anger and all will be well. Late July finds several planets, including Mercury, gathering in your 8th house of mystery. Near Lammas a spirit entity may visit. It wishes to be helpful. During the first half of August, Venus brightens your sector of success and accomplishment. Coworkers appreciate your creativity and breezy personality. Host a picnic or other outing with business associates to deepen important connections. Network.

From September through mid-October your 9th house heats up with a dynamic Mars transit in your sister fire sign of Leo. Always attracted to higher learning, you might enroll in a study program. It's a promising cycle for travel. At the autumnal equinox bless a blue candle. Burn it on the night before your departure to assure a safe journey. October 8 through November 5 Venus will conjoin your Sun. This is a very promising influence for both romance and financial acumen. Make the most of your appearance. Strive to project a desirable first impression. The 1st house of personal image is highlighted. Try a flattering new hairstyle, updated wardrobe, and a smile to work magic in your life. Place a favorite self portrait on the altar at Samhain to honor your body. It is the beautiful temple of your spirit.

Mars causes a stir in your career sector throughout November. There can be some stressful situations professionally. Resist the temptation to indulge in criticism and sarcasm if annoyed. You might inadvertently upset others more than you realize. Frustration and anger must be directed toward making constructive progress. On December 2 the Sagittarius New Moon conjoins your Sun. Set goals to honor your birthday and begin fresh projects. December 5 – 24 Mercury dashes through your birth sign. This is marvelous for travel and for overall decision making. You are moving forward on many levels. At the winter solstice, study seasonal holiday lore to better understand the deeper wisdom it offers.

Retrograde Venus joins Pluto in your money sector in January. Don't overextend financially. Set funds aside to cover an unexpected expense. At Candlemas Mercury joins Neptune in your 4th house of family life. Connect with guardian angel energy for assistance with a complicated domestic situation. Communication is subtle with loved ones during February. Encourage discussion of dreams over breakfast. Dream analysis might provide insight concerning the needs of those closest to you. March finds Jupiter completing its retrograde cycle in your 8th house. The last weeks of winter bring upbeat financial news. An inheritance, investment, tax return, or insurance settlement could be involved.

HEALTH

On May 9 a solar eclipse falls in your 6th house of health. May is a good time to keep up with regular medical check-ups. Taurus, ruler of sound and hearing, is accented. Listen carefully. Casual conversations or broadcasts about health overheard coincidentally offer useful information.

LOVE

You are a wandering free spirit in matters of the heart. All year unpredictable Uranus sparkles in your 5th house of love. Romantic needs are evolving. The lunar eclipse on October 18 initiates some unexpected developments in love, perhaps a change in the status of a relationship.

SPIRITUALITY

A Saturn transit affects your Scorpio-ruled 12th house of the hidden psyche. You can experience an awakening of consciousness during times of quiet reverie and retreat. Spiritual rewards come through charitable work. Focus on what you can offer to help disadvantaged persons or displaced animals.

FINANCE

Pluto in Capricorn impacts your 2nd house of cash flow all year. You're aware of how worldwide economic trends are creating new financial scenarios. June 26 – November 7 and in March 2014 Jupiter will bless your 8th house. Gain comes through unearned income. A partner's money, inheritance, insurance settlement, or other resources add to your security.

# CAPRICORN
The year ahead for those
born under the sign of the Goat
**December 22 – January 19**

Thoughtful, practical, and down-to-earth, Capricorn is ruled by sober Saturn. The responsible and persevering Goat meets challenges and solves problems by combining a strong work ethic with a healthy dose of common sense. Your characteristic bittersweet sense of humor smooths the way.

From the vernal equinox through April 13 variety is truly the spice of life. Your 3rd house is highlighted by Mercury, with Neptune hovering in the background. This promises an interesting daily schedule punctuated by numerous messages and outings. The secret to juggling several ongoing projects successfully is organization. The April 25 eclipse conjoins Saturn in your 11th house. A cycle of new goals and dreams develops. Longtime friends can drift away; a new social circle emerges. Membership in a group or professional association influences your future. On May Eve dedicate a ritual to clarity to assure that you make good choices. Taurus transits play tag in your 5th house of romance throughout May. A loving relationship moves forward. You would enjoy sharing cultural pursuits, crafts, or athletics during leisure hours.

Throughout June, your 7th house sets the pace. Teamwork, compromise, and flexibility are important. Partners have strong feelings concerning plans and ideas. The summer solstice focuses on a commitment ceremony. The June 23 Full Moon in Capricorn offers insights concerning the needs of your nearest and dearest. On July 9 Saturn finishes a retrograde pattern. A sense of completion and freedom surrounds you, cheering the hot, bright days of summer. Venus casts a favorable slant on your 9th house late July through mid-August. This is perfect for long distance travel or for enrolling in a study program. Appreciation of beauty marks Lammastide. Employ spiritual art and music to heighten your connection with the Lord and Lady.

September through early October finds Mars in your 8th house. Hidden facts come to light; a message from the spirit world arrives. Your attitudes and perceptions are in flux. The October 18 eclipse reveals how family dynamics are shifting. A new residence or home remodeling project might be desirable. Progressive Uranus is conjunct the eclipse, so modernization of your surroundings would be pleasing. Mid-October through December 7 a lovely Mars trine blesses you with great vitality. Much can be accomplished; be guided and inspired by your core values. Assume a position of leadership. For Samhain a warrior's costume would be ideal. What about a Valkyrie, Amazon, Civil War soldier, or Hun?

Venus hugs Pluto in Capricorn and both planets conjoin your Sun November 6 – March 5. This exceptionally long aspect promises love and happiness. Your appearance and personality will exude charm, and others will be supportive and helpful. At the winter solstice wear your best holiday finery and bless a clear crystal to wear for charisma. On New Year's Day 2014, the New Moon is in Capricorn. This favors a fresh start. Write a list of wishes and resolutions for the year to come. Early January finds Mercury sharpening your tongue and wit with a quick passage through your birth sign. Gather information; enjoy an impromptu journey near your birthday. The Full Moon on January 15 conjoins Jupiter in your relationship sector. You're ultra proud of a partner's success. A bond strengthens.

February finds many aspects in cardinal signs bombarding your Sun. The pace is lively. Enjoy the moment. Postpone taking on new projects, as they could overwhelm you. March finds both Mars and Saturn turning retrograde, affecting your casual friendships and career prospects. Deep roots related to old times are stirring. To make the best of this situation follow the advice of Confucius who once said, "If you would divine the future, look to the past."

## HEALTH

From the vernal equinox until June 25 Jupiter, the celestial healer, will move through your 6th house of health. Prepare a cleansing spring tonic. Include seasonal fruits and vegetables with meals. This is a wonderful time to facilitate wellness. Health challenges can be overcome.

## LOVE

The May 9 eclipse in Taurus creates excitement and surprises in your 5th house of love while making a favorable aspect to Pluto in Capricorn. All of this aspects your Sun. Prepare for a change of heart. New ideas about love surface. Venus remains in your birth sign a very long time during the autumn and winter months, promising a cycle of popularity and happiness.

## SPIRITUALITY

Neptune, which always attunes to spiritual energies, is in your 3rd house all year. This indicates that short day trips to visit spiritual sites can offer important insights. A local historical walk or ghost tour would be worthwhile. If there is a meditation circle or yoga class meeting in your neighborhood, give that a try. Discuss spiritual perceptions. Casual conversations offer nuances which facilitate your spiritual awakening.

## FINANCE

Your financial sector is ruled by progressive, inventive Aquarius. Seek ways to employ the latest technologies in fulfilling your security needs and desires. Throughout the year Uranus, your fiscal indicator, will square your Sun from the 4th house. Prepare for a financial roller coaster ride. Family members can require extra assistance. Look for ways to reduce expenses related to housing. The very end of winter, after March 6, ushers in a favorable Venus aspect in your 2nd house of cash flow. This promises a financial breakthrough. Rags turn to riches.

# AQUARIUS
The year ahead for those
born under the sign of the Water Bearer
**January 20–February 18**

Broad concepts concern this most liberal and eccentric of birth signs; there is a tendency to dismiss the details as mere minutiae. Ruled by unpredictable Uranus, you are fond of metaphysics, inventions, and novelty. A devoted friend, you're impressed by acts of charity and kindness and will seek to demonstrate humanitarian ideals.

Springtime finds jubilant Jupiter brightening your 5th house of love and pleasure. The good times are in full swing and roll on through the summer solstice. Since the dual sign of Gemini is presiding, a merry romantic dance involving more than one prospect is possible. This influence is exceptionally creative too. Give tangible expression to your original ideas. During the first three weeks of spring you'll be talking and thinking a great deal about money. Mercury moves through your financial sector. You'll seek to balance career goals with family life. A change in the status quo is coming; don't be stubborn. Let matters evolve. All will be well after an adjustment period.

June 1 through mid-July Mars will trine your Sun. You experience an energy boost which makes your workload easier. Outdoor recreation is enjoyable. July 22 brings the first of two Full Moons in Aquarius; this one aspects Saturn. You will be called upon to take on some new responsibilities. Cheerfully demonstrate what you're capable of. A career situation is arising, and a new cycle impacting your professional status unfolds. At Lammastide offer a libation of grape juice to thank the Creator for all you have been given. During August a parade of Leo transits will oppose your birth sign. There is competition afoot. Others can seem unappreciative or preoccupied, especially near the New Moon in Leo on August 6. Adopt a live-and-let-live stance; strike out on your own.

August 20 brings a rare occurrence, the second consecutive Full Moon in Aquarius. Honor the moonlight with an altar of white flowers and silver candles. A dream or meditation brings you important insights concerning completions and new directions. Late August through mid-September finds transiting Venus trine your Sun. Travel and scholarship are harmonious and enjoyable. You connect with an intriguing comrade. A journey or study program can be a part of this. It's an optimum time to write a poem or short story, perhaps for publication. The autumnal equinox arrives with powerful Mars and Saturn aspects. Much is expected of you. Make an effort, and you might rise to professional prominence.

October begins with Mercury entering your career sector, where it will remain until December 4. Think things through carefully if considering a job change. The total eclipse on November 3 evokes an impulsive mood. You are fed up and ready to seek greener pastures. Wait until after Mercury's retrograde is over on November 11 to finalize career decisions. A journey, interview, or conference could impact your situation.

The second week of December begins with Mars entering Libra where it will remain through the end of winter. This is very favorable for your intellectual development and expanding philosophical insights. You'll solve puzzles and acquire information. Your vitality is high, and you'll feel physically warm as the winter solstice nears. Stroll outdoors to celebrate the frosty evening on the longest of nights. Your 12th house is highlighted from late December through mid-January. Appreciation for solitude and peace is present. A volunteer job or charitable endeavor brings satisfaction.

The New Moon in Aquarius on January 30 ushers in fresh enthusiasm and a desire to begin new projects. Mercury retrogrades back and forth between Aquarius and Pisces near your birthday. Business travel is likely. Remember to get both sides of every story. Sort through the facts and finalize decisions after March 1. Venus enters your birth sign on March 6. Happiness, love, and good financial opportunities brighten the final weeks of winter.

## HEALTH

On June 26 Jupiter enters your health sector where it remains through the winter. The most favorable wellness cycle you've experienced in 12 years commences. Mars joins Jupiter July 14 – August 27. That is the time to seek any needed medical care or to begin a fitness program. The New Moon on July 8 and the Full Moon on January 15 are two lunations which reveal important clues concerning how hereditary factors impact your health.

## LOVE

The springtime blesses your love sector with light and airy influences generated by planets transiting Gemini. Intimacy is yours for the asking. Prepare an aromatherapy blend at the vernal equinox with mixed floral essences. Add a tiny garnet to the elixir, and touch the brew to your pulse points. Stroke a drop on a rose-colored candle and ignite the wick to attract true love.

## SPIRITUALITY

The lunar eclipse of May 25 affects your 11th house of friendships; it powerfully aspects mystical Neptune. This ushers in a significant six-month cycle regarding the role that covens and other spiritually focused groups play in your life. You can learn much from others regarding your spiritual path through the autumnal equinox. January favors contemplative inner reflection. A solitary observation is the best way to honor Candlemas.

## FINANCE

Security-oriented Saturn is the co-ruler of Aquarius. Financial acumen is extremely important to your happiness and well-being. Saturn remains in your career sector all year. This emphasizes patience regarding monetary gain. After your birthday the financial outlook brightens.

# PISCES

*The year ahead for those
born under the sign of the Fish*
**February 19 – March 20**

Reserved and silent, the gentle Fish appreciates kindness and longs to trust everybody. Pisces is seldom aggressive, yet has a complex and high voltage emotional nature. Ruled by elusive Neptune, you tend to be restless, whimsical, and visionary.

A Mercury influence at the vernal equinox finds you uncharacteristically talkative. Through All Fools' Day the stars favor a focus on planning and correspondence. Embrace travel opportunities too. The New Moon on April 10 falls in your financial sector and conjoins Mars. Some frustration linked to money matters follows. Consider new strategies for enhancing your security.

During May your 3rd house sets the pace. Stay informed about current events; the news provides valuable perspectives and insights. Educational broadcasts are enjoyable. June finds Venus entering your love sector, where it will favorably aspect Neptune. This highly romantic influence prevails through the summer solstice. A nurturing relationship brings you joy. On the longest day of the year weave a wreath of seasonal herbs and flowers to bless and protect your love.

Throughout July and early August, Mercury and Jupiter will highlight your creative potentials. Pursue a favorite hobby or avocation. It could generate additional income and bring you recognition, even some celebrity status. Love prospects continue to be promising during the long summer days. Travel, perhaps by ship, is likely. Visit an island. Lammastide brings an ecstatic energy boost from a supportive Mars aspect. Dance, your favorite form of exercise, is the perfect way to frolic at the sabbat. Twirl and sway to the music until dawn.

From late August through the autumnal equinox Mercury and the Sun accent partnerships. It's important to communicate well. Listen to what is really being said. The Pisces Full Moon on September 19 brings an awareness of the roles others play in your life. Record dreams. Your spirit guardians may use them as a way to convey important insights. Place a Herkimer diamond in your pillow and burn sandalwood incense in the evening to intensify dream experiences.

The first half of October finds Mars stirring your health sector. Control stress; keep your work environment comfortable and wholesome. The October 18 eclipse affects your finances. Your source of income can go through a shift. Be adaptable and economize. The remainder of October finds Venus in your 10th house of career. This brings pleasant opportunities to combine business with pleasure. Ask coworkers for ideas and assistance. Near Samhain, Mars in Virgo opposes your Sun. Others have plans in mind which involve you. Maintain goodwill by cooperating and consulting. A favorable Pluto aspect encourages fashioning your Halloween costume of vintage or recycled items. Try a steam punk look.

The November 3 solar eclipse highlights your 9th house, turning your attention toward distant shores and imported items. You'll tire of all that has become too comfortable and familiar. This mood continues, supported by transits from Mercury, Saturn, and the Sun, until early December. On November 14 Neptune completes a retrograde cycle. A blockage which has hampered your progress melts away. A goal is about to materialize.

December finds Mars in your 8th house where it remains through the winter. Associates affect your financial situation. Use care regarding joint business enterprises. Estate planning or an inheritance might be in your thoughts. At the winter solstice there is secrecy afoot. Burn a Yule log to push aside dark shadows and invoke the light of truth.

Benevolent Capricorn transits in your 11th house during January bring supportive friendships your way. Seek a mentor to help you select worthwhile goals. The Full Moon on January 15 is magnetic in regard to love. You are at your most attractive. At Candlemas Mercury and Neptune conjoin your Sun. Sacred chanting can be very effective. This is also a favorable influence for dedicating a candle to invoke the help of archangels.

Throughout February you will want to keep a low profile. Your 12th house sets the pace, creating a yen to quietly enjoy your own home. On March 1 the Pisces New Moon favorably aspects Jupiter and Saturn. This is a positive indicator for progress as winter ends. Important obligations are met.

## HEALTH
The Sun rules your health sector. Explore how the healing qualities of the full spectrum light support wellness. If you feel depressed, seasonal affective disorder (inclement weather and too much darkness) might be to blame. The Leo Full Moon on February 14 draws healing energies your way.

## LOVE
At the end of June the most fortunate of planets, Jupiter, begins a year-long transit through your 5th house, the love sector. A genuinely happy cycle for love unfolds. Nurture a cherished relationship. Build a foundation for future happiness.

## SPIRITUALITY
Saturn brings stability to your 9th house of higher consciousness this year. You are seeking spiritual guidance for practical help in resolving problems. Carry a medicine bag of carefully selected stones and herbs. A daily yoga practice helps develop practical insights.

## FINANCE
From the vernal equinox through the summer solstice favorable transits in your 4th house, which rules real estate, indicate that the sale or purchase of property could pave the way to financial freedom. During June a family member's contributions or advice brings welcome financial assistance.

# Sites of Awe

*Haiti and the Baron*

HAITI is truly a country of wonder. The mighty mountains reach up from the sea and create a place where the people claim to be 80% Christian and 100% Voodoo practitioners. I was fortunate enough to visit Haiti a number of times during the 1980s. On one particular trip, I decided to visit the Baron's Cross in the National Cemetery in Port-au-Prince.

As the taxi drives down the main street parallel to the National Cemetery, it is difficult to see anything over the large white wall that surrounds it. My driver takes a left turn and pulls the taxi over to the curb. "Is this where you want to go sir?" "Yes," I answer, "but, how do I get inside?" "You want to go inside? Are you sure, sir?" he asks. After I explain that I am a curious American, he points to the gate in the wall and I ask him to wait for me. The black iron gates marking the opening in the wall are flanked by a number of Haitians standing on each side – probably waiting for friends or family members that had entered the cemetery.

## The Cement-ery

Once inside, I find the cemetery to be quite different from an American cemetery. This one is totally constructed of cement! There are no roads, grass, crushed stone, or plants. It is entirely paved with concrete. The various tombs that inhabit this uncommon place are also constructed of cement or stone. With the exception of the artificial flowers, painted tin decorations, candles and offerings, the entire place is whitewashed. Everything is white.

After getting over the surprise of this eerie site, I make my way a few steps inward away from the men and women at the gate, whose eyes never seem to leave me. There is an uncanny stillness as I walk inside. The sounds of the street seem to fade into the distance and I can only hear the occasional walking of another visitor who has come to pay his solemn respects. I find myself veering left and right through the narrow maze of walkways, always heading in the direction of the center of the cemetery – or so I thought.

### The Baron's Cross

I am not sure how far I have gone, but surely I must have gone off in the wrong direction, as I have still not caught sight of the Baron's Cross. A moment later, I come upon it – both spell-binding and awe inspiring, the Cross is set upon a riser, making it appear even larger. From ground level, it stands about nine feet high, paying tribute to the Baron himself. I stare in wonder as I see the numerous people sitting about. Offerings are laid at the base of the Cross – flowers, candles, fruit, rum, and of course cigars. These people have come to pray to the Baron Samedi – leader of the Ghede and Lord of the Cemetery. There is an overwhelming presence here. It might be called a presence or spirit, but it is undoubtedly here. The next few moments become very personal, and at the time I am quite oblivious to the songs and chants that can be heard around me. No doubt, they are sacred songs and prayers asking the blessing of the dead or of the Baron himself. I am lost in a place where the world of the dead overlaps with the world of the living, and I like this feeling.

As I take a final look at the surroundings, I make a mental note of all that I have seen and experienced. I don't know if I will ever be back to this haunting place, but I will never forget the day I visited the Baron's Cross and the message I received.

The taxi driver is relieved to see me return.

– ARMAND TABER

# Reviews

## BOOKS

*The Elements of Ritual*
by Deborah Lipp

ISBN-10: 073870301X
ISBN-13: 978-0738703015
Paperback: Available through either
Amazon or Barnes and Noble.
List price: $21.95

AS AUTHOR Deborah Lipp points out in the introduction, books for the beginning witch are manifold, thanks to the proliferation of recent interest in the Old Ways. But while most of these books are content to tell you how the practice of witchcraft is carried out, Lipp takes the time to explain why. *The Elements of Ritual* is an easy to comprehend, step-by-step guide to understanding and designing your own cyclical rituals. Thematically built around the four elements of Earth, Air, Fire, and Water, Lipp gently leads the reader through each aspect of casting a ritual circle, making sure to stress the importance of the underlying meaning of each action. Lipp's instruction ranges from the practical mundane (how to keep your energy from flagging during a long spell casting session) to the eminently lofty (how best to harness the confluence of spirits). Lipp's perspective is accessible to the beginner and yet deep enough to prove useful to even the most experienced practitioner.

## MOVIES

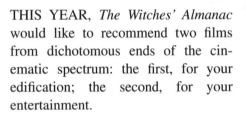

Available through either Amazon or Barnes and Noble.

THIS YEAR, *The Witches' Almanac* would like to recommend two films from dichotomous ends of the cinematic spectrum: the first, for your edification; the second, for your entertainment.

### Cave of Forgotten Dreams

WERNER HERZOG'S documentary *Cave of Forgotten Dreams* is literally a once-in-a-lifetime film. Herzog takes the viewer to southern France, deep into the ancient caves of Chauvet. Access to this cave system has been severely restricted since 1994, when scientists discovered the earliest examples of artistic painting by humans. The French government quickly sealed the caves to protect the paintings from the hot breath and greasy fingers of the general public. Since then, only a small cadre of scientists has been allowed to enter the caves – until Herzog, along with a high definition 3D camera, was granted access to film the amazing scenes for posterity. Once inside the caves, the viewer is treated to a breathtaking gallery of ancient art, rendered in such fine and interesting detail. Herzog's narration is patently offbeat but informative. If you can see the film rendered in three dimensions it is truly astounding; however, this film is worth seeing in any dimension.

### Trollhunter

DIRECTED BY André Øvredal, *Trollhunter* is presented to the viewer as actual found footage from a student film about a bear poacher in Norway. The students track the illegal hunter in an effort to garner an interview and make their names as film makers; what they discover is much more insidious than bear poaching. We won't reveal too much about how the film unfolds, suffice it to say those fond of folklore will find plenty to smile about in this charming romp through troll-infested Norway.

## MUSIC

### Marianne Faithfull

*Horses & High Heels*

Available through either Amazon or Barnes and Noble.

AN ENIGMATIC beauty, Marianne Faithfull is an artist of rare talent. She has journeyed roads less travelled, while simultaneously attracting the attention of industry hit makers. *Almanac* readers with an eye for esoteric ephemera may recall that she appeared as Lilith in Kenneth Anger's occult masterpiece film, *Lucifer Rising. Horses & High Heels*, her eighteenth studio album features a few new songs, as well as some well known covers. If you have a taste for esoteric nostalgia, mixed with hippie sensibility, then you'll be thrilled to know that Marianne is as good as ever. It has earned an honored place on my iPod!

### Richard Thompson

*Live at Celtic Connection*

*Live at the BBC*

Available through either Amazon or Barnes and Noble.

IT IS my distinct pleasure to introduce or reacquaint *Witches' Almanac* readers to the music of Richard Thompson. Twenty-plus albums and CDs after his ground-breaking work with Fairport Convention, Thompson ranks amongst the greatest songwriters and is also an acclaimed guitar player. Two particular items, released in the last year, are, I believe, of particular note:

*The Richard Thompson Band: Live at Celtic Connections* – this DVD of a live performance features an eclectic collection of tasty tunes and showcases the rare talents of this virtuoso performer.

*Live at the BBC* — a box set comprising a complete retrospective of the very best British Country Rock that you will ever hear.

# From a Witch's Mailbox

## Into the Digital Frontier

Are you planning on doing an e-book format of *The Witches Almanac*?

— Jayden D.
Weehawken, N.J.

*An electronic version of some past Almanacs is already available for the Kindle at Amazon.com, for all you paperless netizens. But don't worry, oh ye archaic bibliophiles; the paper edition is still available as well.*

## An Eye for Horus

What's up with the bird on the cover of the last Almanac and why is it there with the Sun?

— Jim H.
Lincoln, Nebraska

*The theme of last year's Almanac was the power of the Sun, so we thought it fitting to depict Horus, the sky god of the ancient Egyptians, since the Sun is an attribute of Horus. Horus is often depicted as a Falcon or a Falcon headed man, hence the bird. Horus's eyes are said to be the Sun and the Moon, and these celestial bodies rise and fall as Horus flies across the sky. The Moon, his left eye, used to be as bright as the Sun, his right. Unfortunately, Horus's left eye was ripped out of its socket by the vengeful Set. Horus's new eye (courtesy of Thoth)*

*worked well enough as a replacement, but it just didn't shine like the original. All thanks to Ogmios MacMerlin for his excellent original artwork.*

## Do-it-yourself Cleaning . . .

I read somewhere something about a recipe for a floor wash, can you give me one?

— Abigail T.
e-mail

*Most commercial cleaning products contain unpronounceable, unheard of chemicals that can make us uneasy, especially if we have small pets or children to worry over. But did you know that common household vinegar has antiseptic, germ-fighting properties? Simply make a solution of 10% vinegar, 90% water and you have a floor wash which is safe, effective, and 100% non-toxic! To add fragrance to your concoction, brew some fragrant tea (such as mint or berry tea) and toss it into the mix. Add some sage or hyssop for an extra boost of cleansing power – while the vinegar removes harmful earthbound germs, sage and hyssop can help clean out more ethereal negative energies.*

## . . . & Do-it-yourself Crafts!

Is there a natural way to color spring eggs?

— Madge B.
Warwick, RI

*There's no need to buy commercial dyes to brighten up your spring eggs – why not celebrate the bountiful colors of spring by looking to nature itself for inspiration? Use fresh vibrant blossoms or the colorful rinds of fruits and vegetables to achieve beautiful subtle colors; even some teas such as chamomile, green tea, hibiscus, and rose hips will impart their hues to your eggs. Some dyes work better than others – for example, beets will turn your eggs a beautiful deep maroon, while green tea imparts a much more muted tone. Experiment with different fruits, vegetables, and teas to find the colors that most inspire you. The easiest way to extract colors from nature is by boiling your natural dyes (be it tea, onion skin, purple cabbage leaves, beet or grape juice, berries, etc.) and your eggs together with a splash of our old friend vinegar. By the time your eggs are hard boiled, they'll also be clad in spring colors!*

## More for the Bibliophiles

Can you recommend a good beginners book on Witchcraft?

– Balthasar
e-mail

The Wiccan Path: A Guide for the Solitary Practitioner *by Rae Beth is an excellent book for those just starting to think about the craft. The book is the result of a correspondence between the author, a seasoned hedge witch, and two friends interested in becoming witches, so the tone is very conversational.* Wheel of the Year: Living the Magical Life *by Pauline Campanelli is a more formal introduction to the practice, outlining the appropriate celebrations and activities month by*

*month. Finally, a classic for the more experienced reader,* Mastering Witchcraft: A Practical Guide for Witches, Warlocks & Covens *by Paul Huson will give practitioners intricate technical and historical knowledge of witchcraft.*

## Let us hear from you, too

*We love to hear from our readers. Letters should be sent with the writer's name (or just first name or initials), address, daytime phone number and e-mail address, if available. Published material may be edited for clarity or length. All letters and e-mails will become the property of The Witches' Almanac Ltd. and will not be returned. We regret that due to the volume of correspondence we cannot reply to all communications.*

The Witches' Almanac, Ltd.
P.O. Box 1292
Newport, RI 02840-9998
info@TheWitchesAlmanac.com
www.TheWitchesAlmanac.com

**Wingfoot Oils and Incense** – *A source for traditional and original incense and oil blends. Serving all of your spiritual needs and made with the finest quality ingredients.*

If we don't have it in our catalog, ask us for it!
Come visit our site at http://www.wingfoot.org/

For free shipping on all orders over $75, use coupon code ALMANAC2013 as thanks for supporting *The Witches' Almanac!*

TM

THE SPEED OF FLIGHT

w i n g f o o t . o r g

### Witchcraft, Paganism & Folklore

*The Cauldron* is widely recognized as a well-respected and leading magazine in the field of modern witchcraft and magic – always interesting, sometimes controversial, but never dull.

Contact: M.A. Howard, BM Cauldron, London WC2N 3XX, England.
www.the-cauldron.org.

## The SILVER WILLOW

### For all your new age, herbal & spiritual needs!

54 Fall River Avenue
Rehoboth, MA 02769
508-336-8813

*We offer a 10 month herbal apprenticeship program.*

**www.TheSilverWillow.com**

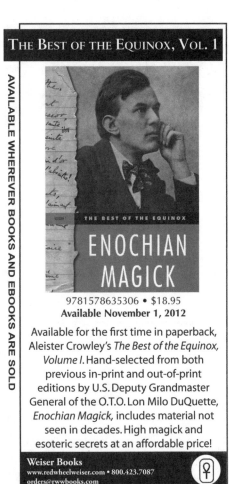

AVAILABLE WHEREVER BOOKS AND EBOOKS ARE SOLD

THE BEST OF THE EQUINOX, VOL. 1

THE BEST OF THE EQUINOX

## ENOCHIAN MAGICK

9781578635306 • $18.95
**Available November 1, 2012**

Available for the first time in paperback, Aleister Crowley's *The Best of the Equinox, Volume I.* Hand-selected from both previous in-print and out-of-print editions by U.S. Deputy Grandmaster General of the O.T.O. Lon Milo DuQuette, *Enochian Magick*, includes material not seen in decades. High magick and esoteric secrets at an affordable price!

**Weiser Books**
www.redwheelweiser.com • 800.423.7087
orders@rwwbooks.com

*The products and services offered above are paid advertisements.*

⌐ CLASSIFIED ⌐

TO: The Witches' Almanac, P.O. Box 1292, Newport, RI 02840-9998

*www.TheWitchesAlmanac.com*

Name_____

Address_____

City_____ State_____ Zip_____

E-mail_____

WITCHCRAFT being by nature one of the secretive arts, it may not be as easy to find us next year. If you'd like to make sure we know where you are, why don't you send us your name and address? You will certainly hear from us.

*The products and services offered above are paid advertisements.*

*Since 1994 Herbs & Arts has served Denver and the region, striving to be a place of healing & sanctuary for the Pagan & Wiccan communities, and all seekers of spiritual living.*

*We live with a simple intention, to put forth compassion, love & gratitude into the universe with the belief that if we can inspire & empower healing and spiritual connection in ourselves and others, the world will change for the better.*

*We make 100's of ritual oils, incenses, & bath salts for all your magickal needs. All of our ritual products are made in sacred space and at specific lunar & astrological times. Our webstore also has over 400 herbs, essential oils and other items to support your connection to spirit.*

*Blessed be.*

# Herbs & Arts

www.herbsandarts.com        Denver, CO        303.388.2544

# The Witchcraft of Dame Darrel of York

Charles Godfrey Leland

*Introduction by Robert Mathiesen*

The Witches' Almanac presents:

- *A previously unpublished work by folklorist Charles Godfrey Leland.*
- *Published in full color facsimile with a text transcript.*
- *Forward by Prof. Robert Mathiesen.*

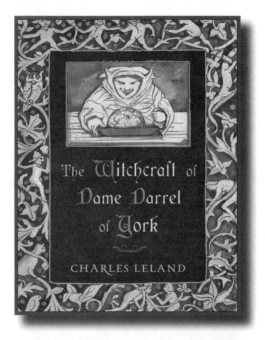

This beautifully reproduced facsimile of the illuminated manuscript will shed light on an ancient tradition as well as provide the basis for a modern practice. It will be treasured by those practicing Pagans, scholars, and all those fascinated by the legend and lore of England.

Standard hardcover edition ($65.00).
Deluxe numbered edition with slipcase ($85.00).
Exclusive full leather bound, numbered and slip cased edition ($145.00).

*For further information visit http://thewitchesalmanac.com/damedarrel.html*

# ARADIA
## GOSPEL OF THE WITCHES
### Charles Godfrey Leland

ARADIA IS THE FIRST work in English in which witchcraft is portrayed as an underground old religion, surviving in secret from ancient pagan times.

• Used as a core text by many modern neo-pagans.

• Foundation material containing traditional witchcraft practices

• This special edition features appreciations by such authors and luminaries as Paul Huson, Raven Grimassi, Judika Illes, Michael Howard, Christopher Penczak, Myth Woodling, Christina Oakley Harrington, Patricia Della-Piana, Jimahl di Fiosa and Donald Weiser. A beautiful and compelling work, this edition has brought the format up to date, while keeping the text unchanged. 172 pages    $16.95

---

## ⪫ *Newly expanded classics!* ⪪

## The ABC of Magic Charms
### Elizabeth Pepper

SINCE THE DAWN of mankind, an obscure instinct in the human spirit has sought protection from mysterious forces beyond mortal control. Human beings sought benefaction in the three realms that share Earth with us — animal, mineral, vegetable. All three, humanity discovered, contain mysterious properties discovered over millennia through occult divination. An enlarged edition of *Magic Charms from A to Z*, compiled by the staff of *The Witches' Almanac.*    $12.95

## The Little Book of Magical Creatures
### Elizabeth Pepper and Barbara Stacy

*A loving tribute to the animal kingdom*

AN UPDATE of the classic *Magical Creatures*, featuring Animals Tame, Animals Wild, Animals Fabulous – plus an added section of enchanting animal myths from other times, other places. *A must for all animal lovers.*    $12.95

✤ a lady shape-shifts into a white doe ✤ two bears soar skyward ✤ Brian Boru rides a wild horse ✤ a wolf growls dire prophecy

**Witches All**

# A Treasury from past editions…

*Perfect for study or casual reading,* Witches All *is a collection from* The Witches' Almanac *publications of the past. Arranged by topics, the book, like the popular almanacs, is thought provoking and often spurs me on to a tangent leading to even greater discovery. The information and art in the book – astrological attributes, spells, recipes, history, facts & figures is a great reminder of the history of the Craft, not just in recent years, but in the early days of the Witchcraft Revival in this century: the witch in an historical and cultural perspective.* Ty Bevington, Circle of the Wicker Man, Columbus, Ohio

*Absolutely beautiful! I recently ordered* Witches All *and I have to say I wasn't disappointed. The artwork and articles are first rate and for a longtime* Witches' Almanac *fan, it is a wonderful addition to my collection.* Witches' Almanac *devotees and newbies alike will love this latest effort. Very worth getting.*
Tarot3, Willits, California

---

## GREEK GODS IN LOVE

Barbara Stacy casts a marvelously original eye on the beloved stories of Greek deities, replete with amorous oddities and escapades. We relish these tales in all their splendor and antic humor, and offer an inspired storyteller's fresh version of the old, old mythical magic.

## MAGIC CHARMS FROM A TO Z

A treasury of amulets, talismans, fetishes and other lucky objects compiled by the staff of *The Witches' Almanac*. An invaluable guide for all who respond to the call of mystery and enchantment.

## LOVE CHARMS

Love has many forms, many aspects. Ceremonies performed in witchcraft celebrate the joy and the blessings of love. Here is a collection of love charms to use now and ever after.

## MAGICAL CREATURES

Mystic tradition grants pride of place to many members of the animal kingdom. Some share our life. Others live wild and free. Still others never lived at all, springing instead from the remarkable power of human imagination.

## ANCIENT ROMAN HOLIDAYS

The glory that was Rome awaits you in Barbara Stacy's classic presentation of a festive year in pagan times. Here are the gods and goddesses as the Romans conceived them, accompanied by the annual rites performed in their worship. Scholarly, light-hearted – a rare combination.

## CELTIC TREE MAGIC

Robert Graves in *The White Goddess* writes of the significance of trees in the old Celtic lore. *Celtic Tree Magic* is an investigation of the sacred trees in the remarkable Beth-Luis-Nion alphabet; their role in folklore, poetry, and mysticism.

## MOON LORE

As both the largest and the brightest object in the night sky, and the only one to appear in phases, the Moon has been a rich source of myth for as long as there have been mythmakers.

## MAGIC SPELLS AND INCANTATIONS

Words have magic power. Their sound, spoken or sung, has ever been a part of mystic ritual. From ancient Egypt to the present, those who practice the art of enchantment have drawn inspiration from a treasury of thoughts and themes passed down through the ages.

## LOVE FEASTS

Creating meals to share with the one you love can be a sacred ceremony in itself. With the witch in mind, culinary adept Christine Fox offers magical menus and recipes for every month in the year.

## RANDOM RECOLLECTIONS
## II, III, IV

Pages culled from the original (no longer available) issues of *The Witches' Almanac*, published annually throughout the 1970's, are now available in a series of tasteful booklets. A treasure for those who missed us the first time around; keepsakes for those who remember.

# News from The Witches' Almanac

*Glad tidings from the staff*

### *"Every Back Issue We Have" SALE*
Until stock runs out, we are offering twenty back issues of *The Witches' Almanac* (1993-2012), a free *Witches' Almanac* book bag and free shipping, all for $100 – over $200 value.

### *Calling all Spells*
*The Witches' Almanac* staff is collecting spells for an upcoming book. If you have interest in participating, send your spell to info@TheWitchesAlmanac.com. We will reply to writers whose spells we choose. Happy Spellcrafting!

### *Helping Witches Down Under*
In our effort to reach our extended family in the southern hemisphere, *The Witches' Almanac* plans on adding a page or two to our next *Almanac* issue to address the changes in the calendar for their region. Keep an eye peeled for this new addition.

### *New Storefront!*
We have finally found a store-front home at The Troll Shop in East Greenwich, RI. Here you will find all of our titles, products, clothes, jewelry and more. Pay us a visit – browse through the large collection of trolls and imports during select store hours. The shop is also the home of a psychic reader. Call for hours.
**The Troll Shop** • 88 Main Street, Greenwich, RI • 401-884-9800

### *Social Networking*
Keep in touch with *The Witches' Almanac* via facebook (http://www.facebook.com/pages/The-Witches-Almanac) and twitter (http://twitter.com/#!/Witches Almanac).

### *Going Green*
In our ongoing effort to help Mother Earth, *The Witches' Almanac* is once again printed on recycled paper! Help our campaign – sign up for our e-mail newsletter at http://TheWitchesAlmanac.com/emailform/html.

# Order Form

Each timeless edition of *The Witches' Almanac* is unique.
Limited numbers of previous years' editions are available.

| Item | Price | Qty. | Total |
|---|---|---|---|
| 2013-2014 The Witches' Almanac | $11.95 | | |
| 2012-2013 The Witches' Almanac | $11.95 | | |
| 2011-2012 The Witches' Almanac | $11.95 | | |
| 2010-2011 The Witches' Almanac | $11.95 | | |
| 2009-2010 The Witches' Almanac | $11.95 | | |
| 2008-2009 The Witches' Almanac | $10.95 | | |
| 2007-2008 The Witches' Almanac | $9.95 | | |
| 2006-2007 The Witches' Almanac | $8.95 | | |
| 2005-2006 The Witches' Almanac | $8.95 | | |
| 2004-2005 The Witches' Almanac | $8.95 | | |
| 2003-2004 The Witches' Almanac | $8.95 | | |
| 2002-2003 The Witches' Almanac | $7.95 | | |
| 2001-2002 The Witches' Almanac | $7.95 | | |
| 2000-2001 The Witches' Almanac | $7.95 | | |
| 1999-2000 The Witches' Almanac | $7.95 | | |
| 1998-1999 The Witches' Almanac | $6.95 | | |
| 1997-1998 The Witches' Almanac | $6.95 | | |
| 1996-1997 The Witches' Almanac | $6.95 | | |
| 1995-1996 The Witches' Almanac | $6.95 | | |
| 1994-1995 The Witches' Almanac | $5.95 | | |
| 1993-1994 The Witches' Almanac | $5.95 | | |
| The Witchcraft of Dame Darrel of York, clothbound | $65.00 | | |
| Aradia or The Gospel of the Witches | $16.95 | | |
| The Horned Shepherd | $16.95 | | |
| The ABC of Magic Charms | $12.95 | | |
| The Little Book of Magical Creatures | $12.95 | | |
| Greek Gods in Love | $15.95 | | |
| Witches' All | $13.95 | | |
| Ancient Roman Holidays | $6.95 | | |
| Celtic Tree Magic | $7.95 | | |
| Love Charms | $6.95 | | |
| Love Feasts | $6.95 | | |
| Magic Charms from A to Z | $12.95 | | |
| Magical Creatures | $12.95 | | |
| Magic Spells and Incantations | $12.95 | | |
| Moon Lore | $7.95 | | |
| Random Recollections II, III or IV (circle your choices) | $3.95 | | |
| *SALE* 20 back issues with free book bag and free shipping | $100.00 | | |
| The Rede of the Wiccae | $22.95 | | |
| Keepers of the Flame | $20.95 | | |
| **Subtotal** | | | |
| **Tax** (7% sales tax for RI customers) | | | |
| **Shipping & Handling** (*See shipping rates section*) | | | |
| **TOTAL** | | | |

| BRACELETS | | | |
|---|---|---|---|
| Item | Price | Qty. | Total |
| Agate, Green | $5.95 | | |
| Agate, Moss | $5.95 | | |
| Agate, Natural | $5.95 | | |
| Agate, Red | $5.95 | | |
| Amethyst | $5.95 | | |
| Aventurine | $5.95 | | |
| Fluorite | $5.95 | | |
| Jade, African | $5.95 | | |
| Jade, White | $5.95 | | |
| Jasper, Picture | $5.95 | | |
| Jasper, Red | $5.95 | | |
| Lapis Lazuli | $5.95 | | |
| Malachite | $5.95 | | |
| Moonstone | $5.95 | | |
| Obsidian | $5.95 | | |
| Onyx, Black | $5.95 | | |
| Opal | $5.95 | | |
| Quartz Crystal | $5.95 | | |
| Quartz, Rose | $5.95 | | |
| Rhodonite | $5.95 | | |
| Sodalite | $5.95 | | |
| Tigereye | $5.95 | | |
| Turquoise | $5.95 | | |
| Unakite | $5.95 | | |
| **Subtotal** | | | |
| **Tax** (7% for RI customers) | | | |
| **Shipping & Handling** *(See shipping rates section)* | | | |
| **TOTAL** | | | |

| MISCELLANY | | | |
|---|---|---|---|
| Item | Price | Qty. | Total |
| Pouch | $3.95 | | |
| Matches: *10 small individual boxes* | $5.00 | | |
| Matches: *1 large box of 50 individual boxes* | $20.00 | | |
| Natural/Black Book Bag | $17.95 | | |
| Red/Black Book Bag | $17.95 | | |
| Hooded Sweatshirt, Blk | $30.00 | | |
| Hooded Sweatshirt, Red | $30.00 | | |
| L-Sleeve T, Black | $20.00 | | |
| L-Sleeve T, Red | $20.00 | | |
| S-Sleeve T, Black/W | $15.00 | | |
| S-Sleeve T, Black/R | $15.00 | | |
| S-Sleeve T, Dk H/R | $15.00 | | |
| S-Sleeve T, Dk H/W | $15.00 | | |
| S-Sleeve T, Red/B | $15.00 | | |
| S-Sleeve T, Ash/R | $15.00 | | |
| S-Sleeve T, Purple/W | $15.00 | | |
| Postcards – set of 12 | $3.00 | | |
| Bookmarks – set of 12 | $1.00 | | |
| Magnets – set of 3 | $1.50 | | |
| Promo Pack | $7.00 | | |
| **Subtotal** | | | |
| **Tax** (7% sales tax for RI customers) | | | |
| **Shipping & Handling** *(See shipping rates section)* | | | |
| **TOTAL** | | | |

## SHIPPING & HANDLING CHARGES

**BOOKS:** One book, add $4.00. Each additional book add $1.50

**POUCH:** One pouch, $2.00. Each additional pouch add $1.50

**MATCHES:** Ten individual boxes, add $2.50.
One large box of fifty, add $6.00. Each additional large box add $3.50.

**BOOKBAGS:** $4.00 per bookbag.

**BRACELETS:** $2.00 per bracelet.

Send a check or money order payable in U. S. funds or credit card details to:

The Witches' Almanac, Ltd., PO Box 1292, Newport, RI 02840-9998

(401) 847-3388 (phone) • (888) 897-3388 (fax)
*Email: info@TheWitchesAlmanac.com • www.TheWitchesAlmanac.com*